the complete guide to baby sign language

the complete guide to
BABY
SIGN
LANGUAGE

200+ SIGNS FOR YOU AND BABY
TO LEARN TOGETHER

lane rebelo

ILLUSTRATIONS BY BORIS STOILOV

ROCKRIDGE
PRESS

For general information on our other products and services or to obtain technical support, please contact our Customer Care Department within the United States at (866) 744-2665, or outside the United States at (510) 253-0500.

Rockridge Press publishes its books in a variety of electronic and print formats. Some content that appears in print may not be available in electronic books, and vice versa.

Interior and Cover Designer: Liz Cosgrove
Photo Art Director/Art Manager: Sara Feinstein
Editor: Bridget Fitzgerald
Production Editor: Ashley Polikoff
Photography: All photography used under license from Shutterstock.com.
Author Photo: © Jacquelyn Warner
Illustrations: © Boris Stoilov, 2019

ISBN: Print 978-1-64152-567-1
eBook 978-1-64152-568-8

To my husband, André,
for your support and encouragement,
and to Annie and Clara,
for all you continue to teach me about life and love.

contents

introduction

WELCOME TO *The Complete Guide to Baby Sign Language*! I'm so excited you've decided to continue learning and growing your American Sign Language (ASL) vocabulary for even more fun—and for more communication opportunities with your little one.

In my first book, *Baby Sign Language Made Easy*, I walked readers through everything they need to know to get started with baby sign language, including 101 of my favorite signs to use with babies and toddlers. And yet, there was still so much more I wanted to share! This complete guide will add more than 175 new signs to your tool kit, which means a *lot* more opportunities for signing, playing, and learning together with your growing child.

You may be coming to this book having already read *Baby Sign Language Made Easy*, or maybe not. Either way, I've got you covered. This book was created with beginners in mind as well as more advanced signers looking to continue building up their signing skills. In this book, you'll find a review of the best signs to start with as well as more challenging signing vocabulary and strategies.

It's been more than 10 years since I started my baby sign language program, Tiny Signs®, and I continue to love teaching classes and workshops, both in person in the Boston area as well as online. One of my favorite things about working with young children and teaching baby sign language is that each child is unique, so the signs that are effective and motivating for one child might be completely different from the next—which makes it so interesting! One toddler might want to sign about animals or vehicles all day long, while another toddler loves to communicate about food. As parents and educators, we can pay attention to children's individual interests and then focus in on related signs so we can seize learning opportunities when they arise.

My hope is that this book will inspire you and help you take your baby sign language experience to the next level, so you'll feel confident using more sophisticated signs in your conversations with your little one. There is a whole world of language and discovery awaiting you—so much more to learn and do together!

HOW TO USE THIS BOOK

This book is written for anyone looking to use ASL vocabulary to enhance and nourish early communication and learning with children. You may be looking to facilitate conversation with your preverbal infant or toddler, or perhaps you're using sign language to help a child with a speech delay or other communication challenge to express her needs (see ASL with Special Needs, page 9). Regardless of the age or developmental level of the child you want to communicate with, this book will help make that possible.

In chapter 1, you'll find a summary on how to get started with baby sign language, including my top tips for successful signing. You'll also get an overview of signing with children with special needs. This chapter is both a good refresher for those already having success with sign language, and the perfect starting place for a total beginner.

If you haven't read *Baby Sign Language Made Easy*, be sure to read chapter 2, which covers what I call the Foundation Signs. You'll learn my formula for picking the right signs to start with as well as the 15 signs that I believe every parent and caregiver should learn. Other basics you'll learn in this chapter include 20 more signs to round out your baseline baby sign vocabulary, plus fingerspelling the alphabet in ASL and counting to 10 on just one hand. At the end of this chapter and throughout the book, you'll find easy-to-follow instructions on how to use songs, books, and activities to teach and practice signing.

In chapter 3, you'll build your practical sign language vocabulary by learning more signs for your daily routines (page 46), food and drink signs (page 56), and some advanced signs for toys to add to your playtime (page 68). If you're already signing and have a good handle on the basics, this is a great place to start.

Chapter 4 is where we really start to dive into more advanced vocabulary, covering signs for emotions, like **BRAVE** (page 87) and **FRUS-TRATED** (page 87). You'll also learn signs for common action words, like **JUMP** (page 94), **SWIM** (page 96), and **RUN** (page 96). This chapter also covers a wide range of opposite words, which offer fun learning opportunities for older toddlers and preschoolers. I've included two songs to help your little one learn the difference between **BIG** (page 103) and **LITTLE** (page 103), **UP** (page 101) and **DOWN** (page 101), and many other opposites.

Chapter 5 takes us out and about to learn signs about home and family (page 114), community (page 124), and school (page 141). We'll also explore some signs to help keep us healthy and safe (page 133)—think how useful it would be if your toddler could point out what hurts rather than just fuss and cry, leaving you wondering what's wrong. As in other chapters, I'll also take you through some wonderful picture books and the perfect songs to practice the signs you've learned, plus some advanced ASL lessons.

Lastly, chapter 6 covers some of my personal favorites, like colors (page 154), animals (page 163), and nature signs (page 176). In fact, you may discover that some of your child's favorite signs in the book end up coming from this chapter! You'll have so much fun signing

ALLIGATOR (page 165), **GORILLA** (page 166), and **PENGUIN** (page 167), for example. And when you head outside to play, you can talk to your child about the **GREEN** (page 157) **GRASS** (page 180) and the **WHITE** (page 160) **CLOUD** (page 178) up in the **SKY** (page 179).

At the end of this book, you'll find resources you can use to help continue practicing and growing your ASL communication skills, plus an alphabetical index of all the signs in this book. And if there's a sign you're looking for that you don't see in this book, be sure to visit my website, TinySigns.net, where you'll find a video dictionary with hundreds of signs for every baby and toddler's particular needs and desires.

So, whether you're just getting started with baby sign language or are ready to take the next step with more advanced vocabulary and strategies, you'll find just what you're looking for in the pages ahead. Let's get started!

1

Baby Signing & Beyond

IS BABY SIGN LANGUAGE just for babies? For preverbal infants, signing is useful and fun, but the usefulness of signing definitely doesn't stop once little ones start walking! In fact, signing can be a lifesaver for chatty toddlers (what the heck are they saying, anyway?) and an incredible learning tool for curious preschoolers. In this chapter, I'll start by filling you in on all the many ways signing can help as your little one grows from a baby to a toddler to a "big kid" in preschool—and even into kindergarten! You'll learn my best tips for signing with little ones as well as how you can continue developing your signing vocabulary as your child grows and develops. I'll explain the differences between baby sign language, which uses vocabulary from American Sign Language (ASL), and true ASL. And you'll learn how signing benefits kids with speech delays or other communication challenges. Are you ready? Let's go!

BABY SIGN LANGUAGE AND ASL

If this book uses ASL, why it is called "baby sign language?" Isn't baby sign language just made-up signs?

These are great questions! In fact, I am often asked about this in my classes, workshops, and teacher trainings.

In some learning resources, the term *baby sign language* refers to the practice of using arbitrary or made-up gestures or simplified versions of sign language with babies. However, baby sign language can also refer to actual signs from ASL that are used with hearing children. In this book, all of the signs used are ASL signs.

ASL is a beautiful language used by a half-million people in the United States and Canada. It's important to know that ASL is not simply English conveyed in signs—it has its own unique grammar and syntax. A simple example of how ASL differs from English can be shown with the following question: "What is your name?" In English, the question is both spoken and written the same way. In ASL, the question is communicated with signs in the following order: **NAME**, **YOU**, and **WHAT**? Clearly, the use of words in ASL is quite different from English!

When we pair individual ASL signs with spoken language, the end result becomes something that is related to, but different from, true ASL. In this book, we will not be creating ASL sentences. Instead, we will pair individual ASL signs with spoken words, using key words to communicate. While this is not formal ASL, it is a very effective hybrid of two languages for communicating with young children whose speech skills are still developing.

If you enjoy learning the signs in this book, I strongly encourage you to learn more about ASL and the Deaf community. You'll find some good resources to start with in the back of the book (Resources, page 187).

SIGNING THROUGH THE STAGES

When people think of baby sign language, they often think it's, well, just for babies. But the reality is that most babies don't start signing until they are in the 8- to 12-month age range. Some start even later. In fact, many parents and caregivers don't realize just how useful signing can be until they've got a very frustrated toddler on their hands!

Parents of toddlers often ask me, "Is it too late to start signing?" My answer is always an emphatic *no*! Really, anyone who has difficulty expressing their thoughts and feelings verbally can benefit from signing. Like with other developmental milestones, such as sitting up, crawling, and walking, every child is different when it comes to signing. Some babies might make their first sign as early as 5 months old, while others might not start until after their first birthday, and that's perfectly fine! No matter when you start, or when your baby starts signing back, signing can be an indispensable tool for communicating with toddlers, preschoolers, and older children with special needs.

In particular, toddler speech can be notoriously difficult to decipher, causing frustration all around. Signing along with speech can be really useful for clarifying those hard-to-understand words. When paired with the sign for **BALL** (page 22), a "buh buh" vocalization will make it crystal clear that your little one is talking about his ball and not a **BALLOON** (page 75), a **BOOK** (page 22), or a **BOAT** (page 129).

Another benefit of signing with an older child is that they tend to pick up signing very quickly. Signing with an infant takes patience as you wait for that first sign back, but toddlers and preschoolers tend to learn signs quickly—sometimes even signing back on the first day you introduce a new sign!

One thing I love about signing with little ones is that you can witness how creative they get as they use their signs. As a young toddler, my daughter signed **BATH** (page 19) to express her excitement (and confusion) about the new water table we got for her to play with on the deck. Even signs used incorrectly can start a conversation about a new topic. We filled the water table, grabbed a few toys, and signed **WATER** (page 17) and introduced the sign

for **BOAT** (page 129). She quickly learned that this new item was a **TOY** (page 69) for her to play with, not a new bathtub, as she initially thought, and would sign **BOAT** whenever she wanted to play with it.

Signing can also be a wonderful way to involve toddlers and preschoolers with a new sibling. A new big sister or big brother who is still very young is likely not able to provide much hands-on help with the new baby. Being enlisted with the important job of teaching and modeling sign language can help them feel involved in the new baby's care and more connected to their new sibling.

Preschoolers and young school-age children love using sign language in the classroom because it allows them to be more involved in learning. Signing along to a story being read by a teacher allows children to actively and physically participate instead of just sitting and listening. Signing is useful for nearly all children because it is engaging for many learning types. The needs of visual, auditory, physical, verbal, and social learners can all be met through signing, because signing engages both the eyes and the ears and involves physical movement as well as interpersonal connection. Some teachers even report that signing creates a quieter and more peaceful classroom environment, as young students look to their teacher for visual clues instead of the teacher having to speak loudly to be heard.

Some research suggests that using sign language in the early childhood classroom can even be beneficial for building prereading skills. In her book, *Dancing with Words: Signing for Hearing Children's Literacy*, Marilyn Daniels discusses the many benefits of using sign language, including better letter and sound recognition, improved spelling, and higher reading levels, in classrooms where teachers incorporated ASL into their daily lessons.

TEACHING MORE (AND MORE!) SIGNS

Things start to get really exciting once your little one starts signing. There are so many things to identify, label, and talk about in the world around you! You might even feel a little overwhelmed, especially if learning sign language is new to you, too. Not to worry! Take it one step at a time. If you don't know the sign for something, make a note to look it up and introduce it at your next opportunity. You won't learn all the signs all at once. Like with learning any new language, your ASL vocabulary will grow one sign at a time, and that's just fine.

So how quickly should you introduce new signs? That really depends on you and your child. You can introduce new signs as opportunities present themselves. If you are heading out to run errands, perhaps you can plan to introduce the sign for **STORE** (page 126) or **LIBRARY** (page 126) that day. You can also follow your child's lead and look up signs for things he seems interested in. If he likes opening and closing the cabinet doors, then teaching him the sign for **DOOR** (page 116) might be fun. Start introducing the sign for **COLORS** (page 155) as you read a book about colors or **DRAW** (page 145) with **CRAYONS** (page 150). You can introduce a new sign each day or each week, or even multiple signs in one day if you're both on a roll! Just follow your child's lead and do the best you can. Before you know it, you'll be using more signs than you can keep track of!

Here are five important tips to keep in mind as you introduce new signs:

Choose signs based on your child's interests.

This is really my favorite tip. While many resources prescribe certain signs to start with, I have found that parents who choose signs based on their *baby's* interests have more success with signing. To pick good starter signs, spend a little time observing your child. What does your little one seem interested in? Do you have a **DOG** (page 21) or a **CAT** (page 21) that he loves to pet? Is he obsessed with eating **AVOCADO** (page 63) or playing with a toy **ROCKET** (page 73)? Use your observations to make smart choices of signs that will motivate and excite your child to start signing.

ASL with Special Needs

A number of developmental issues can impact a child's ability to communicate, including speech delay, Down syndrome, autism, and apraxia, to name a few. These developmental challenges can affect a child's ability to speak clearly or even speak at all. Sign language can be a lifesaver for families struggling with the frustration of trying to communicate with a child who is unable to express her needs and wishes because of a disability.

Often, developmental issues are not discovered until a child is well beyond the baby stage, leaving parents wondering if it's too late to take advantage of the benefits of baby sign language. The answer is that it's never too late. Sign language can be used with *any* child, regardless of age, who is unable to form words or be understood via speech. Sign language can serve as a vital tool throughout childhood and into adulthood for any individual with a disability that interferes with their ability to express themselves verbally.

Teaching an older child with special needs to sign can look very similar to teaching an infant or toddler to sign. However, if you're teaching a child with special needs to sign, it's important to adjust expectations for how long it might take the child to start signing based on their unique skills and abilities. Here are some tips for best success:

- Be patient and model the signs you'd like the child to learn, frequently and consistently.

- Slow the signs down and speak clearly so the child has ample opportunity to see and hear the word.

- If the child doesn't object, gently guide their hands to show them how to do the sign themselves.

- Most importantly, be supportive and encouraging.

When looking for a child to sign back, it's important to keep in mind that their version of the sign might be limited by their motor skills and range of motion. Keep your eyes open for any movement that appears to be purposeful and repetitive, and compare it to the signs you've been using in order to decipher what the sign might be.

If your child has developmental challenges, hopefully you have an experienced team of professionals helping you as you work together to support your child's growth and learning. This team might include a speech therapist, occupational therapist, physical therapist, and other specialists. Talk to your child's providers about using sign language to support their budding communication skills and to make sure everyone is working together to support your efforts.

With patience and gentle encouragement, you'll come to celebrate your amazing child's ability to communicate with you using sign language, and you can pat yourself on the back for providing them with a life-giving tool to connect with the world around them!

Always sign and say the word together.

This tip is simple but important. You always want to *say* and *sign* the word at the same time. The ultimate goal when signing with hearing children is to facilitate and encourage communication skills and speech development, and saying the word each time you sign it will support their developing speech and language skills.

Always sign in context.

When you're introducing a new sign, always use it in a context that naturally supports learning the new sign. For example, sign **MILK** (page 16) when your baby is feeding, sign **BALL** (page 22) when your baby is holding a ball, sign **DOG** (page 21) when the dog is visible in the room, and so on. Signing in context will help your baby make the connection between the sign, word, and object more quickly. Once your child establishes the meaning of a particular sign/word, you can use the sign any time!

Sign in your child's line of sight.

It can be tricky to get your little one to look at you when you're trying to show them a new sign. When introducing a new sign, you'll want to put yourself and especially your hands where your little one can see them. One strategy you can try is to make an interesting

sound to get your child to look at you. For example, if he is looking at a car, you can say "Beep beep! Vroom vroom!" to make your baby turn to look at you. Once he's looking at you, say and sign **CAR** (page 23) before he looks away. Mission accomplished!

Have fun!

If you want to succeed with signing, the absolute best thing you can do is make it fun. Signing should be playful and silly, never a chore. If you're feeling tired and grumpy, or your little one's having an "off" day, skip the signing and try again when you're both feeling better. When signing is incorporated into playtime, story time, and songs, your baby will be eager to get in on the action. Throughout this book, I'll offer some fun ways to incorporate sign language into familiar songs, books, and simple activities.

Signing is fun and easy, especially when you feel confident that your efforts will pay off. Following these practical tips will prevent confusion and help your baby get the hang of signing in no time.

Signs with Shared Meaning

One way that sign language differs from spoken language is that in ASL, multiple concepts can often be conveyed with just one sign. For example, in English, we use the words *eat*, *food*, *meal*, and *snack* to express a variety of meanings. In ASL, however, the sign **EAT** (page 16) conveys the meaning for *all* of these words. Therefore, it's fine to use the sign **EAT** when you say any of the words that share the same concept. Using the same sign with different spoken words that have similar meanings won't confuse your child. In fact, it will help to build her vocabulary by exposing her to additional words, while illustrating the similar or shared meaning through the use of a familiar sign.

Likewise, it's perfectly fine to use one sign with various spoken words that have similar meanings. For example, it's okay to sign **BED** (page 18) or **SLEEP** (page 51) when saying the following phrases to your little one:

*You look so **sleepy**.*

*Do you want to go **night-night**?*

*That's the doggy's **bed**!*

*Shhhh, the baby is **sleeping**.*

Your child will learn that these words share similar meaning when you use a familiar sign with a variety of spoken words, and this will help speed up the learning process. Pretty cool, right?

2

Foundation Signs

LIKE BUILDING A STURDY HOUSE, creating a rock-solid foundation is an essential first step for success with baby sign language. In this chapter, we'll cover the signs that will serve as the groundwork for your growing sign language vocabulary.

First, we'll start with 15 of my most highly recommended signs to start signing, based on my years of teaching sign language to parents and young children. You can't go wrong with any of the Foundation Signs covered in this chapter. Why? Because these signs are either very practical or very motivating and fun! I recommend you master them and use them often. Next, we'll cover 20 more basic signs that I love using with babies and toddlers. These signs are covered in my first book, *Baby Sign Language Made Easy*, so if you've worked through that already, this can be a useful review. If you are starting with this book, you'll want to begin here and get the hang of these first!

Once you've mastered the very basic vocabulary, you'll learn how to sign the alphabet in American Sign Language (ASL). This might feel like jumping into the deep end with advanced signing, but it's actually a great place to get started. Here's why: Many signs in the book are made with the handshapes you'll learn in the ASL alphabet. For example, right in this chapter, you'll see that **WATER** (page 17) is made with a *W* handshape, **POTTY** (page 19) is made with a *T* handshape, and **BUBBLES** (page 24) is made with two *O* handshapes.

Also, signing individual letters, also known as fingerspelling, can be a fun and tangible way for toddlers and preschoolers to start to learn their letters. You can start with the first letter of your child's name and build from there with frequently used words.

Counting in sign language is also a lot of fun. Did you know that in ASL, you can count from 1 to 10 on just one hand? While some of the numbers in ASL are familiar and intuitive, like **ONE** (page 40) and **TWO** (page 40), the others might surprise you! As you learn, you'll have fun singing and counting with songs you'll find in this book, like "Ten Little Dinosaurs" (page 42) and "Five Little Monkeys Swinging in a Tree" (page 174).

Let's dive in and get started with the signs that will lay the groundwork for your sign language success!

USEFUL AND PLAYFUL

One of the most surprising things I've learned in my years of teaching baby sign language is that sometimes the best signs to start with are *not* necessarily the most obvious choices.

When starting out, most parents begin with what I call *useful signs*. You'll find eight of my favorite useful signs in this chapter: **MILK** (page 16), **EAT** (page 16), **WATER** (page 17), **MORE** (page 17), **ALL DONE** (page 18),

BED (page 18), **BATH** (page 19), and **POTTY** (page 19).

Useful signs will make life with little ones a whole lot easier, because your baby will be able to tell you when she is hungry, sleepy, or even needs a diaper change. Another great thing about useful signs is that you can turn to them many times throughout the day—at every feeding, changing, and nap. This gives you lots of chances to practice signing to your baby and lots of opportunities for your little one to see and learn the signs.

However, while these useful signs are very practical, they often are not the signs I see parents having the most success with early on. In fact, after more than a decade of teaching baby sign language, I've learned that an invaluable trick to get babies signing quickly is to incorporate some *playful signs* when you first get started.

Playful signs are important because they work with your baby's interests and curiosity, and they motivate them to start signing. You'll find that there are so many things your baby is eager to "talk" to you about! You'll find seven of my favorite playful signs in this chapter: **CAT** (page 21), **DOG** (page 21), **BOOK** (page 22), **BALL** (page 22), **CAR** (page 23), **LIGHT** (page 23), and **BUBBLES** (page 24). Using some thoughtfully chosen playful signs will make a huge difference in how quickly your baby signs back!

useful signs

milk

Open and close your dominant hand a few times.

✱ **Memory tip**
It's as if you're milking a cow.

☺ **When to use the sign**
If you think your baby is getting ready for a feeding, you can sign **MILK** and ask, "Do you want some **MILK**?" You can reinforce the sign further by signing and saying it while your little one is drinking milk, whether bottle-feeding, breastfeeding, or drinking from a cup.

👁 **What to look for**
Your little one's sign for **MILK** might look like she's waving to you. If her hand is touching her body when she signs **MILK**, it might look like she's scratching an itch.

eat

Bring your fingers and thumb together and tap them to your lips a few times.

✱ **Memory tip**
It's like you're putting food into your mouth.

☺ **When to use the sign**
EAT is a great sign to introduce when your baby starts eating solid foods. Sign **EAT** when you suspect your baby is getting hungry and while he is eating. You can also sign **EAT** if he is watching you or a pet eat.

👁 **What to look for**
Your baby might sign this by sticking his finger (or even his whole hand) in his mouth. He might also pat his face or head.

✿ **Similar signs**
The signs for **EAT** and **FOOD** are the same, so you can use this sign interchangeably with both spoken words.

water

Make a *W* handshape (page 39) and tap it on your chin twice.

✱ Memory tip
W is for water.

☺ When to use the sign
Sign **WATER** when your little one starts drinking water from a sippy cup. You can also sign **WATER** when giving her a bath or if you see water, whether it be a faucet running, a small puddle, a fountain, or a large lake.

👁 What to look for
Babies and most toddlers don't yet have the fine-motor control to form the *W* handshape for this sign, so they will likely sign this by tapping all fingers or just their pointer finger to the chin.

more

Bring your fingers and thumb together on both hands and then tap the tips of your fingers together twice in front of your body.

✱ Memory tip
It's like you're adding things together each time your fingertips touch.

☺ When to use the sign
MORE is often used when babies are eating: "Do you want **MORE**?" This causes some babies to think that **MORE** is the same as **FOOD** (page 16), and they will start to sign **MORE** whenever they are hungry. To avoid this confusion, use it in a variety of contexts, signing **MORE** when you are doing anything your baby enjoys, such as singing, bouncing, playing peek-a-boo, and even getting belly kisses!

👁 What to look for
Little ones might sign **MORE** by clapping their hands or banging their fists together. Or they might touch their pointer finger to their opposite palm.

all done

Start with your hands open and palms facing you, and then twist your wrists so your palms are facing out. Repeat this motion twice.

✴ Memory tip
It's like you're brushing something away from you.

☺ When to use the sign
Use this sign whenever you wrap up an activity with your little one. You can ask, "Are you **ALL DONE**?" when you think he is done eating. Remember to sign and say **ALL DONE** when you're about to take him out of the high chair, car seat, or bathtub. Before you know it, he will be letting you know when he's had enough by signing **ALL DONE** instead of fussing. You can also use this sign when you say "finished" or "the end."

👁 What to look for
Baby might sign this by waving or flapping one or both hands or by sweeping his hands from side to side.

bed

Tilt your head to the side and rest it on the palm of your open hand.

✴ Memory tip
It's like you're resting your head on a pillow.

☺ When to use the sign
Say and sign **BED** whenever your baby is acting sleepy and every time you put her down for a nap and at bedtime. She will make the connection with the sign and start to let you know when she's feeling tired.

👁 What to look for
Baby might just tilt her head to her shoulder, with or without her hand.

bath

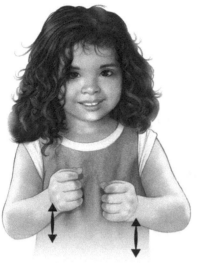

Make a fist with both hands and gently rub your chest up and down.

✳ Memory tip
It's like you're washing your body in the bath.

☺ When to use the sign
Sign **BATH** when you start running the water for a bath. During bath time, if you're using one hand to support your baby, you can modify the sign by doing it with your other hand on either yourself or the baby.

👁 What to look for
It might look like your baby is wiping his body with open hands.

potty

Make a *T* handshape (page 39) with your dominant hand and shake it slightly from side to side.

✳ Memory tip
T stands for *toilet*. However, with babies and toddlers, this sign is often paired with the word *potty* or similar words. It's up to you which spoken word you use with this sign.

☺ When to use the sign
POTTY is a great sign to introduce when little ones begin potty training.

👁 What to look for
At first, this sign might look like a little wave of the fist.

playful signs

cat

Pretend to pinch your cheek with your thumb and pointer finger and pull outward. You can do this sign with one or both hands.

✱ Memory tip
It's like you're showing off your cat whiskers.

☺ When to use the sign
Sign **CAT** when you see a kitty in real life or in a picture. If you have a cat, your baby might be looking at it when you're trying to show her how to do the sign, so try signing **CAT** while holding the kitty. If your cat doesn't mind, you can even gently sign **CAT** on the kitty's face!

👁 What to look for
It might look like your baby is brushing her face with her fingertips or grabbing at her face.

dog

Pat your thigh a few times.

✱ Memory tip
It's like you're calling a dog to come to you.

☺ When to use the sign
Sign **DOG** when your pet is within sight. If you don't have a dog, sign **DOG** when you see one in the neighborhood or when visiting friends or family with one. You'll also find lots of dogs in children's books!

👁 What to look for
Your little one might pat his leg or tummy.

book

Place your hands flat together and then open them outward.

✳ **Memory tip**

It's like you're opening a book.

◎ **When to use the sign**

Let your little one hold a board book while you talk about it. Ask, "Are you reading the **BOOK**?" and "Do you want me to read the **BOOK** to you?" Sign **BOOK** any time you are reading together!

👁 **What to look for**

Your little one might sign **BOOK** by making one large clapping motion or by clasping her hands together.

ball

Curve all the fingers of both hands and bring them toward each other a few times in front of your body.

✳ **Memory tip**

It's like you're showing the shape of an invisible ball.

◎ **When to use the sign**

Balls are a fun and easy way to engage little ones in play. You can get a plush ball for a younger baby and a bouncy one for an older child. Pass the ball back and forth. Sign **BALL** while the little one is holding it. You can even do a modified version of the sign for **BALL** while holding the ball in one hand: Either do half of the sign with your free hand or sign with your free hand on the ball.

👁 **What to look for**

Babies might sign **BALL** by knocking their fists together or clapping. My younger daughter signed **BALL** by touching her closed fist to her opposite open hand.

car

Hold your fists in front of your body with palms facing each other and move them up and down alternately in a circular motion.

✳ Memory tip
It's like you're turning the steering wheel of a car back and forth.

☺ When to use the sign
Sign **CAR** when you're getting in the car, when you're out for a walk and see cars zooming by, and when you see cars in a book. Capture your little one's attention by making fun noises, like "beep beep" and "vroom vroom," when signing **CAR**.

👁 What to look for
Your little one might wave both hands up and down together (with hands open or closed in fists) instead of alternately.

light

Touch all your fingers together and lift the back of your wrist up above your head. Open and close your fingers a few times.

✳ Memory tip
Opening your fingers is like light rays shining down on you.

☺ When to use the sign
Introduce this sign by turning the light off and then on again, either with a lamp or light switch. Turn the light on and say and sign **LIGHT**. Once your baby starts signing **LIGHT**, you'll realize that just about everything has a light!

👁 What to look for
Baby's version of **LIGHT** might look a lot like the sign for **MILK** (page 16), but most babies raise their arm when they sign **LIGHT**. If you're not sure which sign it is, pay attention to your baby's gaze and behavior. Is he looking at you, eager for a feeding? Or is he looking at something with a light on it?

bubbles

Make O handshapes (page 39) with both hands, then open them as you alternate raising each hand.

✱ Memory tip

It's like bubbles floating up into the air and popping.

◷ When to use the sign

Babies love bubbles, so this is a really fun and motivating sign to teach. Most babies will naturally reach up and try to touch the bubbles, which is a great opportunity to cheer them on even though they may not be making the sign. As they reach for the bubbles, you can say, "That's right! **BUBBLES**! Good job signing. Catch the **BUBBLES** with your hands. Pop!"

👁 What to look for

It might look like your baby is waving or signing **MILK** (page 16) or **LIGHT** (page 23) with both hands.

more basic signs to know

mom

With an open hand, tap your thumb on the side of your chin a few times.

mom (alternate)

✱ Memory tip

In ASL, all the signs for females (**GIRL** [page 121] and **AUNT** [page 118]) are done on the lower half of the face, and signs for males (**BOY** [page 121] and **UNCLE** [page 119]) are done on the top half of the face. One way to remember this is that men are generally taller than women.

☺ When to use the sign

Sometimes it's easier for someone other than the mom to teach this sign. Try introducing this sign when someone else is caring for the baby by looking at a picture or signing **MOM** when she walks into the room.

✿ Similar signs

If your family has two moms, or a mom and a stepmom, you can use this alternate version to differentiate the other mom: Touch the thumb of your open hand to the side of your chin and wiggle your fingers a little bit.

dad

With an open hand, tap your thumb on the side of your forehead a few times.

dad (alternate)

✳ Memory tip

As mentioned earlier, in ASL, all the signs for males (**BOY** [page 121] and **UNCLE** [page 119]) are done on the top half of the face, and signs for females (**GIRL** [page 121] and **AUNT** [page 118]) are done on the lower half of the face.

⏱ When to use the sign

Just like with **MOM** (page 26), sometimes it's easier for someone other than the dad to teach baby this sign.

✿ Similar signs

If your family has two dads, or a dad and a stepdad, you can use this alternate version to differentiate the other dad: Touch the thumb of your open hand to the side of your forehead and wiggle your fingers a little bit.

baby

Cradle your arms in front of you and swing them gently from side to side.

✳ **Memory tip**

It's like you're rocking a baby to sleep.

◉ **When to use the sign**

Sign **BABY** when you see or hear a baby when you are out and about. You can also use this sign for toy babies and dolls.

◉ **What to look for**

It might look like your baby is hugging herself or twisting from side to side.

i love you

Hold your hand up with your palm facing forward and your thumb, pointer, and pinky fingers extended.

✳ **Memory tip**

This handshape is a combination of the ASL signs for *I* (page 38), *L* (page 38), and *Y* (page 40), which stands for I-L-Y: **I LOVE YOU**.

◉ **When to use the sign**

Sign **I LOVE YOU** anytime you want, especially when parting ways or when saying goodnight.

◉ **What to look for**

This is a tricky handshape, so babies often do the sign with their whole hand or just the pointer finger extended. I usually add a little shake to this sign—if you do this, too, your baby will probably shake her hand while signing.

please

Rub your flat hand in a circular motion on your chest.

✳ Memory tip
It's like you are rubbing your heart because you want something so much.

◷ When to use the sign
Teach your baby the sign for **PLEASE** by modeling it yourself when you want him to give you something. Or, if he wants something, you can ask him to "say **PLEASE**" and pause a moment before giving the desired object. Don't withhold things for long, though—you don't want to frustrate your baby.

👁 What to look for
Babies often look like they are wiping or rubbing their chest when they sign **PLEASE**.

thank you

Place the fingers of your flat hand on your chin, then move your hand away.

✳ Memory tip
It's like returning the favor when someone gives you something.

◷ When to use the sign
Sign **THANK YOU** to your baby whenever she hands you something or does something you request (like sit down). With time, she will get the idea and sign **THANK YOU** when you give her something!

👁 What to look for
Your baby might touch or tap her mouth, which could look like she's signing **EAT** (page 16).

❀ Similar signs
The sign for **GOOD** is similar to **THANK YOU**. However, when signing **GOOD**, the hand moving away from your chin lands on your opposite open palm.

help

Place your dominant hand in a thumbs-up shape on your opposite palm, then lift them together slightly.

✳ **Memory tip**
It's like your bottom hand is helping lift your top hand.

◎ **When to use the sign**
Ask, "Do you need **HELP**?" when you see her struggling or getting frustrated. In time, baby will let you know she needs **HELP** . . . instead of having a meltdown!

👁 **What to look for**
Baby might look like she is clasping her hands and bouncing them together.

play

Make a *Y* handshape (page 40) with both hands and twist them away from each other.

✳ **Memory tip**
Think of your pinky and thumbs as little kids running all over the place and having a great time.

◎ **When to use the sign**
PLAY is a great sign to use when your baby is in a good mood and you are having fun together. Use this sign when he has a toy or you are playing with him. You can say something like, "You are having so much fun **PLAYING** with that shape sorter! This toy is fun to **PLAY** with!"

👁 **What to look for**
The *Y* handshape is tricky, so your baby might just twist or shake his fists or pointer fingers excitedly.

train

Start with your nondominant hand in a *U* handshape (page 39) with palm facing down. Make another *U* handshape with your dominant hand and slide those fingers back and forth on the opposite two fingers.

✴ Memory tip
It's like your bottom fingers are the track and your top fingers are the train.

☺ When to use the sign
Whenever you find the opportunity to talk about trains with baby—when playing with a toy, reading a book, or maybe while watching a real train go by—say and sign **TRAIN** and add a cheerful "choo choo!" to the interaction.

👁 What to look for
Baby might rub his pointer fingers together or slide his whole hand over the opposite hand.

happy

With your hand in front of you, palm facing toward you, brush your chest upward a few times.

✴ Memory tip
It's like happy feelings are rising up from your heart.

☺ When to use the sign
When using signs for emotions, be sure that your facial expression matches the feeling you're communicating. So when you sign **HAPPY**, be sure to smile!

👁 What to look for
It might look like your baby is patting or rubbing his chest or belly.

music

Swing your dominant hand back and forth over the forearm of your nondominant hand.

✳ Memory tip
It's like you're conducting an orchestra.

☺ When to use the sign
You can sign **MUSIC** when you're listening to music, while singing to your baby, or even if the ringtone on your phone plays a tune. You can also sign **MUSIC** each night when you sing a lullaby.

👁 What to look for
Baby will likely wave or swing one or both arms back and forth. It might look similar to her sign for **ALL DONE** (page 18), so pay attention to context to determine which sign it is.

✿ Similar signs
The sign for **MUSIC** is the same as the sign for **SING**, so you can use this sign with both spoken words.

tree

Place your nondominant hand parallel to the floor, palm facing down. Then place the elbow of your dominant hand on your opposite hand, palm facing forward and fingers open. Then twist your open hand back and forth a few times.

✳ Memory tip
It's like tree branches blowing in the wind.

☺ When to use the sign
You can sign **TREE** while outdoors watching the leaves blow in the wind, while looking at trees through windows at home, or when you see trees in storybooks.

👁 What to look for
Baby might look like he is reaching up and waving or twisting his hand.

moon

Make a modified C handshape (page 38) with just your pointer and thumb and touch it to your cheek, then move it up and away from your face.

✳ Memory tip
It's like you're placing the crescent moon up in the sky.

☺ When to use the sign
The sign for **MOON** can be used when reading bedtime stories, like *Goodnight Moon (page 54)*, *Kitten's First Full Moon*, and *Papa, Please Get the Moon for Me*. Of course, you can also sign **MOON** if you see the real thing in the night sky!

👁 What to look for
It might look like your baby is pointing at the sky.

cracker

Make fists with both hands and knock the fist of your dominant hand twice on the elbow of your nondominant arm.

✳ Memory tip
It's like you are "cracking" wheat to make crackers.

☺ When to use the sign
You can use the sign **CRACKER** for any salty or crunchy snack food. If your little one is like most babies, this will quickly become a favorite sign.

👁 What to look for
Many babies sign **CRACKER** by knocking their fist on their opposite hand or wrist.

banana

Extend the pointer finger of your nondominant hand. With your dominant hand, press your fingertips together and move them from the top to the bottom of your opposite pointer finger.

✳ Memory tip

It's like you are peeling a banana.

☺ When to use the sign

Sign **BANANA** while your little monkey watches you cut or mash bananas, and sign it again while she is enjoying her banana.

👁 What to look for

Baby might sign **BANANA** by brushing her pointer fingers or whole hands together.

mouse

With your pointer finger, brush the side of the tip of your nose a few times.

✳ Memory tip

It's like a mouse's nose twitching.

☺ When to use the sign

Lots of children's books feature mice, such as *Goodnight Moon* (page 54) and *If You Give a Mouse a Cookie*. Make a game of finding the mouse on each page by asking, "Can you find the **MOUSE**?"

👁 What to look for

Baby might poke at his face with his pointer finger or brush his nose with his whole hand.

sheep

With your dominant hand, open and close your pointer and middle fingers like scissors as you move your hand up the opposite arm.

✳ Memory tip
It's like you're shearing the wool off a sheep.

◉ When to use the sign
Sign **SHEEP** when playing with farm animal toys, spotting sheep out in nature, or singing a song with a sheep in it, like "Mary Had a Little Lamb," which is featured at the end of chapter 5 (page 148).

◉ What to look for
It might look like your baby is brushing or rubbing her fingers against her arm.

monkey

With all of your fingers, scratch both of your sides in an upward motion a few times.

✳ Memory tip
It's just like a silly monkey scratching itself.

◉ When to use the sign
This sign is lots of fun to do with exaggerated monkey noises and facial expressions. You can also sign **MONKEY** when singing "Five Little Monkeys Swinging in a Tree" (page 174) with your baby.

◉ What to look for
Baby will surely look like a little monkey when doing this sign!

bear

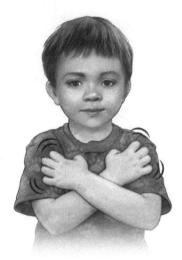

Cross your arms and scratch your shoulders with your fingers bent.

✳ Memory tip

It's like a bear scratching itself with its big bear claws.

◎ When to use the sign

Sign **BEAR** when playing with a teddy bear or reading a book like *Brown Bear, Brown Bear, What Do You See?*

◉ What to look for

Baby might look like she is scratching her chest or belly or giving herself a hug.

dinosaur

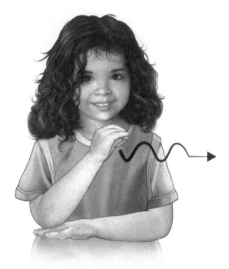

Touch all your fingers to your thumb and move your arm in a heavy up and down motion across the space in front of your body. You can hold your nondominant arm across your body to support this sign if you like, but it's optional.

✳ Memory tip

It's like a big dinosaur lumbering slowly along.

◎ When to use the sign

Sign **DINOSAUR** and roar like a dinosaur when playing with dino toys, singing a song (like the one on page 42), or reading a book like *Oh My Oh My Oh Dinosaurs!* or *How Do Dinosaurs Go to Sleep?*

the alphabet
and numbers

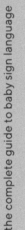

Make a fist with palm facing out and thumb pointing up at the side.

A

Make a flat hand with palm facing out, fingers touching, and thumb tucked in.

B

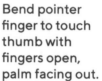

Curve your hand into a *C* shape.

C

Curve all fingers to touch thumb except pointer, which is extended up.

D

Let all fingertips rest along thumb with palm facing out.

E

Bend pointer finger to touch thumb with fingers open, palm facing out.

F

Close hand in a fist with pointer finger and thumb pointing to the side, palm facing in.

G

Close hand in a fist with pointer and middle fingers pointing to the side, palm facing in.

H

Close hand with pinky finger pointing up and palm facing out.

I

Draw a *J* in the air with pinky finger.

J

Raise pointer and middle fingers up in a *V* shape with thumb tucked into the base of the *V*.

K

Raise pointer finger up and thumb to the side to make an *L* shape with palm facing out.

L

M
With palm facing out, fold first three fingers over thumb, which is holding down pinky.

N
Place first two fingers over thumb, which is holding down pinky and ring finger, with palm facing out.

O
Touch all fingers to thumb to make an O shape.

P
Point pointer and middle fingers down in a *V* shape with thumb tucked into the base of the *V*.

Q
Close hand in a fist with pointer finger and thumb pointing down.

R
Twist pointer and middle fingers together with palm facing out.

S
Close hand in a fist with thumb over closed fingers and palm facing out.

T
Close hand with thumb tucked between first two fingers and palm facing out.

U
Point pointer and middle fingers up, touching, with palm facing out.

V
Point pointer and middle fingers up and spread into a *V* shape with palm facing out.

W
Point first three fingers up and spread into a *W* shape with palm facing out.

X
Close hand in a fist with pointer finger up and bent, palm facing out.

Y

Close hand with thumb and pinky extended, palm facing out.

Z

Draw a *Z* in the air with pointer finger.

1

Close hand with pointer finger pointing up and palm facing either in or out.

2

Point pointer and middle fingers up and spread into a *V* shape with palm facing either in or out.

3

Spread pointer finger, middle finger, and thumb open and extended with palm facing either in or out.

4

Point all fingers up and spread open with thumb tucked in, palm facing either in or out.

5

Open hand wide with palm facing either in or out.

6

Touch pinky finger to thumb, with remaining fingers spread open and palm facing out.

7

Touch ring finger to thumb, with remaining fingers spread open and palm facing out.

8

Touch middle finger to thumb, with remaining fingers spread open and palm facing out.

9

Touch pointer finger to thumb, with remaining fingers spread open and palm facing out.

10

Make a thumbs-up gesture with one hand and give it a little shake.

SIGNING FUN

Sign and Read: *Chicka Chicka Boom Boom* by Bill Martin Jr. and John Archambault

I believe this is the absolute best book for teaching the alphabet to little ones! In this book, the lowercase letters of the alphabet are personified as frisky children who all dare each other to climb to the top of a coconut tree. Things get a little messy as the letters all fall down, but fortunately some uppercase grown-ups come to the rescue! You'll be able to practice your fingerspelling as you read the text and point out the colorful letters in the illustrations. There's also a board book version of this book, called *Chicka Chicka ABC*, for younger readers.

Key Vocabulary

TREE, p. 32   **FALL DOWN,** p. 94   **MOM,** p. 26

DAD, p. 27   **UNCLE,** p. 119   **HELP,** p. 30

CRY, p. 84   **MOON,** p. 33   **BED,** p. 18

Sign and Sing: "Ten Little Dinosaurs"

There are lots of songs to practice counting with your little one, including "Five Little Monkeys Swinging in a Tree" (page 174). However, this song is my favorite because children can really learn the sequence of counting from 1 to 10 *and* counting backward from 10 to 1, as well. You can make this song about any animal you want—"Ten Little Elephants," "Ten Little Crocodiles," or just about anything, really! I like to make it about dinosaurs because the syllables sound just right to me, but sing about whatever will be the most fun for you and your little one. You can sign just the numbers if you want to keep it as simple as possible.

Key Vocabulary

DINOSAUR, p. 36   LITTLE, p. 103   ONE, p. 40

TWO, p. 40   THREE, p. 40   FOUR, p. 40

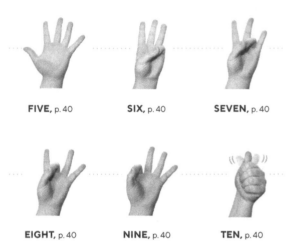

FIVE, p. 40   SIX, p. 40   SEVEN, p. 40

EIGHT, p. 40   NINE, p. 40   TEN, p. 40

(Sung to the tune of "Ten Little Fingers")

ONE little, **TWO** little, **THREE** little **DINOSAURS**

FOUR little, **FIVE** little, **SIX** little **DINOSAURS**

SEVEN little, **EIGHT** little, **NINE** little **DINOSAURS**

TEN little **DINOSAURS** all lined up.

TEN little, **NINE** little, **EIGHT** little **DINOSAURS**

SEVEN little, **SIX** little, **FIVE** little **DINOSAURS**

FOUR little, **THREE** little, **TWO** little **DINOSAURS**

ONE little **DINOSAUR** all alone.

3

Throughout
the Day

DAILY ROUTINES ARE a great place to start introducing sign language to your baby. Things you do regularly each and every day provide natural opportunities for repetition, helping your little one to become more familiar with signing and practice signing herself!

In this chapter, we'll explore three key areas that provide tons of opportunities to sign together: daily routines, food, and toys. You'll also find fun and easy songs set to familiar tunes and books that you can use to reinforce your growing sign language vocabulary and help make learning more enjoyable.

Signs for daily routines will include things like getting **READY** (page 47) each **MORNING** (page 52) before you start your **DAY** (page 52). You'll also learn how to sign **SLEEP** (page 51) and **NIGHT** (page 53) so you can add those to your end-of-day routines, as well.

You'll also learn many new food signs, including ones for fruits, veggies, and more! Mealtime is a great time to sign because you have good eye contact with your little one in his high chair, and you can introduce new signs for foods as you offer them. Your little one will be thrilled when he can let you know he wants more of his favorite food! What do you think it will be? Perhaps it will be **AVOCADO** (page 63) or maybe **BERRIES** (page 59). Or who doesn't love **ICE CREAM** (page 65)?

Lastly, we'll cover a bunch of fun toys you can incorporate into your daily playtime with your little one. Playtime is a fantastic time to introduce new signs, when your little one is fed, rested, and motivated to play and learn. Does she have a favorite **TOY** (page 69)? In this section, you'll learn the signs for all kinds of playthings, including **BALLOON** (page 75), **DOLL** (page 72), and even **DRAGON** (page 74)!

my day and routines

ready

Make *R* handshapes (page 39) with both hands and shake them slightly from side to side.

✳ Memory tip
It's like you're shaking with excitement to get started!

◷ When to use the sign
When it's time to leave the house or start an activity, ask your child, "Are you **READY**?" Use the tone of your voice to show excitement when you're getting ready to do something fun.

✵ Similar signs
READY is also signed with both *R* hands moving out and away from each other once or moving together from left to right.

again

Start with your dominant hand slightly bent with palm up. Flip your dominant hand over so that the fingertips land in the upturned palm of your opposite hand.

✳ Memory tip
Think of asking someone to put something in your hand again.

◷ When to use the sign
You can use **AGAIN** as an alternative to the sign for **MORE** (page 17) if you prefer. This sign also means "repeat" and "do over." A fun way to use this sign is at the end of singing "The Itsy Bitsy Spider" when the spider goes up the spout **AGAIN**. Once your child gets the hang of this sign, watch for it to appear at the end of a merry-go-round ride or other fun activity.

◉ What to look for
It might look like your baby is clapping or patting one hand on the other.

pacifier

Touch your pointer finger and thumb together in front of your mouth.

✳ Memory tip

It's like you're putting a pacifier in your mouth.

◷ When to use the sign

We called my daughter's pacifier a "binky," but I've also heard it called *"paci," "dummy," "soother,"* and so on. You can pair this sign with whatever name you call it in your family.

👁 What to look for

Your baby might touch his mouth with a pointer finger or whole hand.

shower

Lift your dominant hand over your head with all your fingertips touching, and open and close your fingers twice.

✳ Memory tip

It's like your hand is the showerhead and your fingers show the water turning on.

◷ When to use the sign

If your child enjoys a shower more than a bath, use this sign when it's time to take a shower.

👁 What to look for

Your baby might open and close his hand in a similar motion as the sign for **MILK** (page 18) or **LIGHT** (page 23).

wash hair

Move your open hands with bent fingers back and forth at the sides of your head.

✳ Memory tip

It's like you're scrubbing your hair with shampoo.

◉ When to use the sign

Pretend to wash your own hair and then your little one's hair as you say and sign **WASH HAIR**.

◉ What to look for

It might look like your baby is trying to mess up her hair or wipe something from her face or head.

soap

Wipe the fingertips of your dominant hand on the palm of your opposite hand twice.

✳ Memory tip

It's like you're rubbing a bar of soap to make lather.

◉ When to use the sign

It's fine to use the sign for **SOAP** whether using bar or liquid soap. You can also use this sign together with the sign for **WASH HANDS** (page 137).

◉ What to look for

It might look like your baby is rubbing his hands together or trying to wipe off his hands.

towel

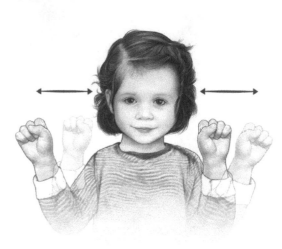

Start with both hands in S handshapes (page 39) at your shoulders and move them side to side in unison.

✱ Memory tip

It's like you're holding an imaginary towel and drying your back.

☺ When to use the sign

Sign **TOWEL** when it's time to dry off from the **BATH** (page 19) or **SHOWER** (page 48) or after you **WASH HANDS** (page 137).

👁 What to look for

It might look like your baby is making a gesture for "hooray!"

✤ Similar signs

You can also do this sign with one hand higher than the other, so the imaginary towel is at a slight angle.

brush hair

With a closed fist, move your hand from the top of your head downward two times.

✱ Memory tip

It's like you're holding an imaginary brush and brushing your hair.

☺ When to use the sign

You can use the sign **BRUSH HAIR** when you are brushing your own hair, your little one's hair, or even your pet's fur.

👁 What to look for

It might look like your baby is rubbing her head or pulling at her hair.

✤ Similar signs

The sign for **COMB HAIR** is done with the same motion, but with the hand open and fingers bent, like a comb.

sleep

Start with your relaxed dominant hand in front of your forehead and move it downward to your chin. Bring your fingers together and close your eyes as your hand moves downward.

✳ **Memory tip**
It's like you're showing the transition from being awake to being asleep.

☺ **When to use the sign**
You can sign **SLEEP** when it's time for bed or a nap or when you are asking your little one if he is sleepy.

👁 **What to look for**
Your baby might slide his whole hand or just a finger down his face.

*My younger daughter would drag her pointer finger down her face to sign **SLEEP**. She would also sign **SLEEP** when her baby doll's eyes closed.*

pillow

Place your relaxed hands on one side of your head with palms facing each other and move them toward each other twice.

✳ **Memory tip**
It's like you're feeling the fluffiness of a pillow under your head.

☺ **When to use the sign**
Make this one fun by pretending to have a very fluffy and comfy pillow to rest your head on as you pretend to take a nap.

👁 **What to look for**
It might look like your baby is signing **BED** (page 18) if she rests her head on her hands.

morning

Place your nondominant hand with the palm facing down on the inside of your opposite elbow and then lift your dominant hand upward with the palm facing up and toward you.

✳ Memory tip

It's like the sun rising up from the horizon.

◷ When to use the sign

Greet your little one with the sign as you say **GOOD** (page 109) **MORNING**! When you pair this sign with **EAT** (page 16)—**EAT-MORNING**—it means "**BREAKFAST**."

day

Place the elbow of your dominant arm on the back of your opposite hand with the pointer finger of your dominant hand pointing up. With the pointer finger extended, move your dominant hand down so that your arm lies flat on your opposite arm.

✳ Memory tip

It's like the sun moving across the sky throughout the day.

✿ Similar signs

Do the first part of this sign with a *B* handshape (page 38) and tap your dominant elbow on the back of your opposite hand to sign **NOON**. If you sign **EAT** (page 16) and **NOON**, that means "lunch." Use the sign for **DAY** in the "Good Morning, Good Night" song (see page 55).

night

Hold your nondominant arm in front of your body with palm down. Bend your dominant hand and bring it down on top of your opposite hand.

✻ Memory tip

It's like the sun dropping below the horizon at the end of the day.

☺ When to use the sign

When you pair this sign with **EAT** (page 16)—**EAT-NIGHT**—it means "**DINNER**." Use the sign for **NIGHT** in the "Good Morning, Good Night" song (see page 55).

SIGNING FUN

Sign and Read: *Goodnight Moon* by Margaret Wise Brown

Is there any children's book more beloved than *Goodnight Moon*? This classic bedtime story will lull your little one to sleep with gentle rhymes as the main character, a little bunny, says "good night" to all the items in his bedroom. As you add signs to your story time, you can use as many or as few signs as you feel comfortable with. An easy way to get started is to introduce the sign for **MOUSE** and spend a little time searching for the mouse on every page that shows the "great **GREEN** room." From there, add more signs as your signing vocabulary and your little one's interests grow.

Key Vocabulary

GREEN, p. 157   PHONE, p. 71   RED, p. 155

BALLOON, p. 75   MOON, p. 33   BEAR, p. 36

CHAIR, p. 117   CAT, p. 21   HOUSE, p. 115

MOUSE, p. 34   BRUSH HAIR, p. 50   NIGHT, p. 53

JUMP, p. 94

Sign and Sing: "Good Morning, Good Night"

Singing a simple song as part of your daily routine can be a wonderful way to build fun and easy language-building activities into your day. This tune can be sung cheerfully as you greet your baby each morning or in a quiet, gentle way as you wind down before bedtime. You can use all the signs offered here or just one or two. Do whatever feels right for you!

Key Vocabulary

GOOD, p. 109

MORNING, p. 52

BABY, p. 28

YOU, p. 102

TIME, p. 147

DAY, p. 52

NIGHT, p. 53

SLEEP, p. 51

(Sung to the tune of "Good Night, Ladies" from *The Music Man*)

GOOD MORNING, BABY [sign **BABY**, or insert baby's name and sign **YOU**]

GOOD MORNING, BABY

GOOD MORNING, BABY

It's **TIME** to start our **DAY**.

and

GOOD NIGHT, BABY

GOOD NIGHT, BABY

GOOD NIGHT, BABY

It's **TIME** to go to **SLEEP**.

food and drink

hungry

Start with a C handshape (page 38) in front of your throat and move it down over your chest.

✳ Memory tip

It's like you're moving the food you want from your throat to your belly.

☺ When to use the sign

As you are preparing food for your hungry baby, ask, "Are you **HUNGRY**? You seem really **HUNGRY**! I'm making some **FOOD** (same sign as **EAT**, page 16) for you!"

👁 What to look for

It might look like your baby is wiping his chest.

thirsty

Start with your pointer finger at the top of your throat and slide it down your neck.

✳ Memory tip

It's like you're showing a nice refreshing drink sliding down your dry throat.

☺ When to use the sign

Sign **THIRSTY** when your little one might need a drink. Ask her, "Are you **THIRSTY**? Do you want some **WATER** (page 17)?"

👁 What to look for

Your baby might point to her mouth or wipe her pointer finger or entire hand on her neck and/or chest.

juice

Start with an *I* handshape (page 38) near your face and move it down and inward toward your body.

✳ **Memory tip**
You are drawing the letter *J* for *juice* near your mouth.

◷ **When to use the sign**
Sign **JUICE** to differentiate fruit or vegetable juice from water in a sippy cup.

👁 **What to look for**
It might look like your baby is waving with his pointer finger or whole hand.

fruit

With an *F* handshape (page 38), twist your pointer finger and thumb on your cheek near your mouth.

✳ **Memory tip**
F stands for *fruit* as you make the motion of twisting a piece of fruit off a stem.

◷ **When to use the sign**
Sign **FRUIT** with any fruit purée or a piece of fruit that you don't know the specific sign for.

👁 **What to look for**
Your baby's version of this sign might be done with her pointer finger and look similar to the sign for **CANDY** (page 65).

berry

Touch all the fingertips of your dominant hand to the tip of your pointer finger of your opposite hand, and twist your dominant hand back and forth.

✳ Memory tip
It's like you're picking a berry off the vine.

◉ When to use the sign
You can use this sign for any kind of berry (strawberry, raspberry, etc.) and when reading *The Little Mouse, the Red Ripe Strawberry, and the Big Hungry Bear* by Don and Audrey Wood (page 66).

◉ What to look for
Your baby might clasp her hands and twist or bounce them up and down.

✤ Similar signs
Sometimes, smaller berries, like blueberries, are signed on the pinky finger instead of the pointer finger to indicate their smaller size.

grape

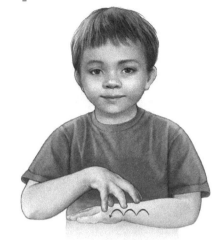

Place the fingertips of your bent dominant hand on your opposite forearm. Tap with your fingertips multiple times, moving down the forearm toward the wrist.

✳ Memory tip
It's like you're showing bunches of grapes on a vine.

◉ What to look for
Your baby might slap his open hand down on his other arm or hand.

raisin

Place the fingertips of an *R* handshape (page 39) on your opposite forearm. Tap with your fingertips multiple times, moving down the forearm toward the wrist.

✳ **Memory tip**
It's like the sign for GRAPE but with an *R* for *raisin*.

👁 **What to look for**
Your baby or young toddler might do this sign with just her pointer finger, as the twisted fingers of the *R* handshape are tricky for little fingers!

❋ **Similar signs**
You can also sign **RAISIN** by combining the signs for **DRY** (page 108) and **GRAPE**: Raisins are **DRY-GRAPES**.

melon

Make a fist with your nondominant hand and then use the middle finger and thumb of your dominant hand to "flick" your closed fist.

✳ **Memory tip**
It's like you're thumping on a melon to see if it's ripe.

🕐 **When to use the sign**
You can use this sign with any kind of melon or gourd, including cantaloupe, honeydew, and even pumpkin!

👁 **What to look for**
Your baby might tap his pointer finger or hand on his opposite hand or arm.

❋ **Similar signs**
Combine the sign for **WATER** (page 17) with **MELON** to sign **WATERMELON**.

vegetable

Place the pointer finger of a *V* handshape (page 39) near your mouth and twist it back and forth.

✳ Memory tip
V is for *vegetable*, just like *F* is for **FRUIT** (page 58).

☺ When to use the sign
Sign **VEGETABLE** when your little one eats veggie purées or vegetables that you don't know the specific sign for.

👁 What to look for
Your baby's version of this sign might be done with his pointer finger and look similar to the sign for **CANDY** (page 65).

peas

Hold the pointer finger of your nondominant hand parallel to the floor, then tap it multiple times with your dominant pointer finger, moving from the base of the finger to the tip.

✳ Memory tip
It's like you're showing all the little peas lined up in a pod.

☺ When to use the sign
Peas are a great finger food! Sign **PEAS** when your little one is enjoying warm peas with a meal, or dried peas as a snack, with or without the pod.

👁 What to look for
Your little one might tap her opposite hand or arm with her finger or whole hand.

corn

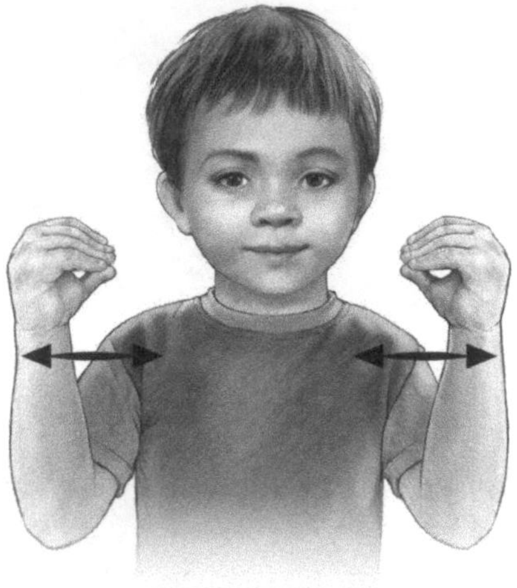

Hold both hands, with all the fingertips of each hand touching, on either side of your face, and move them from side to side together.

✻ Memory tip

It's like you're eating corn on the cob.

When to use the sign

Sign **CORN** when eating corn on the cob or cut corn as finger food.

What to look for

Your baby might wave his hands or touch his face.

tomato

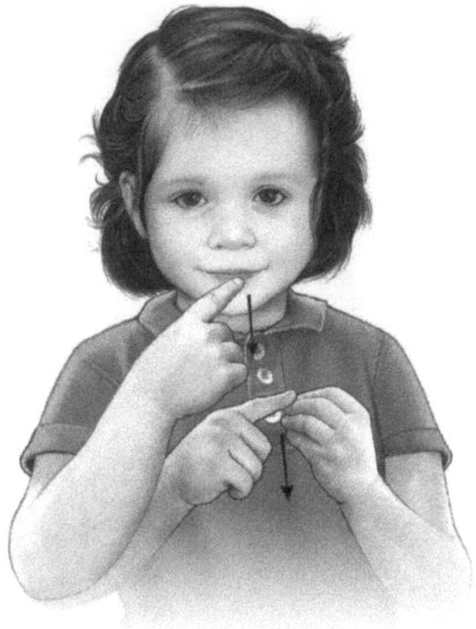

Touch your pointer finger to your lips and slide it down your chin. Then take your pointer and move it downward on the fingertips of your nondominant hand.

✻ Memory tip

This is a modified sign for **RED** (page 155) combined with the motion of slicing a tomato.

Similar signs

This sign is also done with the slicing motion on just the pointer finger of the nondominant hand extended instead of all the fingers.

avocado

Make an *A* handshape (page 38) with your dominant hand and knock it on your opposite palm, then slide it from wrist to fingers.

✳ Memory tip

A is for *avocado*. It's like you are mashing an avocado to make guacamole.

☺ When to use the sign

Avocado is a very popular early food. Use this sign when your baby tries avocado. If he likes the taste, it might be a first sign.

👁 What to look for

Your baby might bang or clap his hands together.

✿ Similar signs

AVOCADO is typically fingerspelled in ASL. However, a number of new signs have been introduced recently as avocados have grown in popularity. As there is not one "official" ASL sign for avocado, you might see it signed in a variety of ways—but fingerspelling always works!

rice

Cup your nondominant hand, palm up, in front of your chest. Make an *R* handshape (page 39) with your dominant hand and move it from your opposite hand to your mouth.

✳ Memory tip

It's like you're scooping rice from a bowl to your mouth.

☺ When to use the sign

You can sign **RICE** for any small grain your baby might eat, including quinoa, spelt, or wild rice.

soup

Cup your nondominant hand, palm up, in front of your chest. Make a *U* handshape (page 39) with your dominant hand and move it from your opposite hand to your mouth.

✳ Memory tip
It's like you're spooning soup from a bowl to your mouth.

☺ When to use the sign
You can sign **SOUP** whenever you're preparing or eating soup of any variety.

cake

Bend all the fingers of your dominant hand and touch the fingertips to the upturned palm of your opposite hand, then lift your dominant hand straight up.

✳ Memory tip
It's like you're showing a cake rising in the oven.

☺ When to use the sign
Sign **CAKE** to represent a slice of cake or a cupcake.

ice cream

Make an *S* handshape (page 39) with your dominant hand and hold it in front of your mouth with palm facing sideways. Move your fist toward your mouth and down a few times in a circular motion.

✳ **Memory tip**
It's like you're holding an ice cream cone and licking it.

☺ **When to use the sign**
You can use this sign for any type of ice cream, including ice cream cones, ice cream sandwiches, or ice cream in a dish.

👁 **What to look for**
Your baby might lick her hand or fist.

✱ **Similar signs**
Sometimes this sign is done with the tongue out slightly.

candy

Touch the tip of your pointer finger to your cheek and twist it a few times.

✳ **Memory tip**
It's like you're pointing to your sweet tooth.

☺ **When to use the sign**
Be careful if your little one learns this sign—he might start asking for **CANDY** all the time!

SIGNING FUN

Sign and Read: *The Little Mouse, the Red Ripe Strawberry, and the Big Hungry Bear* by Don and Audrey Wood

This is the adorable tale of a little mouse with a big problem. The little mouse has a delicious, juicy strawberry, but the narrator has the little mouse shaking with fear about the big, hungry bear that's coming for his delicious berry! What's a scared little mouse to do? No worries—the narrator and mouse come up with the perfect solution. I love using a low, booming voice when the narrator talks about the big, hungry bear to make the story even more fun and dramatic.

Key Vocabulary

LITTLE, p. 103

MOUSE, p. 34

RED, p. 155

BERRY, p. 59

BIG, p. 103

HUNGRY, p. 57

BEAR, p. 36

EAT, p. 16

Sign and Sing: "This Is the Way"

"This Is the Way" is a simple, traditional children's song that you can use with just about any words you can think of (see page 97 for more ideas). It's fun to use at mealtime—substitute different food signs as you introduce new signs and foods. Feel free to swap out the signs in the following lyrics to whatever signs you want to share with your little one.

Key Vocabulary

EAT, p. 16

PEAS, p. 61

HUNGRY, p. 57

JUICE, p. 58

THIRSTY, p. 57

(Sung to the tune of "Here We Go 'Round the Mulberry Bush")

This is the way we **EAT** our **PEAS**

EAT our **PEAS**, **EAT** our **PEAS**

This is the way we **EAT** our **PEAS**

When we're feeling **HUNGRY**.

or

This is the way we drink our **JUICE**

Drink our **JUICE**, drink our **JUICE**

This is the way we drink our **JUICE**

When we're feeling **THIRSTY**.

toy

Make *T* handshapes (page 39) with both hands and twist them away from each other.

✳ Memory tip
T is for *toy*.

☺ When to use the sign
Sign **TOY** when playing with your little one and her favorite toys. You can also sign **TOY** for any toy you don't know the specific sign for.

👁 What to look for
It might look like your baby is waving or flapping her hands.

✳ Similar signs
This sign is similar to the sign for **PLAY** (which is done with two *Y* hands) because they share similar meanings. **TOY** is also commonly fingerspelled in ASL. Make sure to do this sign with both hands—if you do it with just one hand, it's very similar to the sign for **POTTY** (page 19).

slide

Make a *U* handshape (page 39) with your nondominant hand and point the fingertips downward. Make another *U* handshape with your dominant hand and move those fingertips down your opposite fingers to the tips.

✳ Memory tip
It's like a child going down a slide.

☺ When to use the sign
You can sign **SLIDE** when watching older kids or siblings going down a big slide at the playground or when going down a slide at home. While there is also a specific sign for **PLAYGROUND** (page 147), you can sign **SLIDE** to ask your child if she wants to go to the playground and play on the **SLIDE**.

share

Hold your flat nondominant hand in front of your body with your thumb pointing up. Swing your flat dominant hand back and forth above the opposite hand in the space between the thumb and fingers.

✳ Memory tip
It's like you're dividing something in half, with some for you and some for me.

☺ When to use the sign
Sharing is a concept that preschoolers (and some adults!) struggle with. If your baby is still little, use this sign with realistic expectations—this concept can take time to master. A great way to teach the idea of sharing is if you have something your baby wants, perhaps some food: Sign and say, "Do you want to **SHARE** my food with me? I like **SHAR-ING**!" and give him a small portion of what you have.

game

Make two thumbs-up gestures with palms toward your body, and knock the backs of your fingers together twice.

✳ Memory tip
It's like two opponents coming together.

☺ When to use the sign
Sign **GAME** when your little one is old enough to play simple board games, like *Candy Land* and *Chutes and Ladders*. You can also use the sign **GAME** when playing peek-a-boo and hide-and-seek.

👁 What to look for
Your baby might clap her hands or bang her fists together.

puzzle

Make two sideways thumbs-up signs, palms facing down, and move your hands up and down alternately.

✳ Memory tip

It's like you're pushing puzzle pieces into place.

☺ When to use the sign

You can sign **PUZZLE** for a baby-friendly wood puzzle, a complex jigsaw puzzle, or anything in between.

phone

Make a *Y* handshape (page 40) with your thumb at your ear and your pinky near your mouth.

✳ Memory tip

This one's easy—you probably already do this motion, like you're talking on the phone.

☺ When to use the sign

Sign **PHONE** when your baby is grabbing at your cell phone or playing with a toy phone.

👁 What to look for

Your baby might hold his pointer finger or whole hand to the side of his head.

When my daughter signed **PHONE***, it looked the same as the sign for* **BED** *(page 18).*

doll

Make an *X* handshape (page 39) with your dominant hand, and brush your bent pointer finger down your nose a few times.

✴ Memory tip
It's like you're pointing out your cute little doll nose.

⊙ When to use the sign
Sign **DOLL** when playing with a baby doll or Barbie dolls or when you see a doll in a book you are reading.

⊙ What to look for
Your baby might point to her nose or face.

puppet

Open and close your dominant hand next to your face.

✴ Memory tip
It's like you're opening and closing the mouth of a sock puppet.

⊙ When to use the sign
Sign **PUPPET** for hand puppets or marionette-style puppets. You can also use the sign for puppets on television shows like *Sesame Street*.

⊙ What to look for
It might look like your baby is waving bye-bye.

✸ Similar signs
You can sign **PUPPET** with one or both hands.

rocket

Make an *R* handshape (page 39) with your dominant hand and place it on the back of your opposite hand with the *R* pointing up. Move your *R* hand up and away from your nondominant hand.

✳ Memory tip

It's like a rocket blasting off into space.

◉ When to use the sign

Make fun sound effects as your rocket blasts off and your baby will likely do the same!

◉ What to look for

Your baby might "blast off" by moving his pointer finger up above his head.

monster

Curve all of your fingers of both hands and hold them at the sides of your face. Press your hands forward a few times and make a fun or silly face.

✳ Memory tip

It's like a scary monster is coming to get you!

◉ When to use the sign

Sign **MONSTER** for silly creatures in movies and books that can't be identified as a familiar animal. Have fun roaring and growling like a "scary" monster when you do this sign.

◉ What to look for

Your little one might really get into this one and make a big, scary monster. Watch out!

dragon

Start with your dominant hand in front of your mouth with fingertips touching and pointing away from you, then move your hand forward away from your face and wiggle your fingers.

✱ **Memory tip**
It's like flames shooting out of a dragon's mouth.

☺ **When to use the sign**
There are some wonderful picture books, like *Dragons Love Tacos* by Adam Rubin and Daniel Salmieri, that you can use this sign with.

👁 **What to look for**
Your child might look like she's reaching out to tickle you!

clown

Bring the fingers of your dominant hand close to the thumb and tap them twice to your nose.

✱ **Memory tip**
It's like you're showing the big red nose of a clown.

☺ **When to use the sign**
Sign **CLOWN** when you see a clown in a book or show or if you have a toy clown.

👁 **What to look for**
Your baby might point to or tap his nose or face.

We had a jack-in-the-box with a clown that popped up, and my daughter learn to sign **CLOWN** *as we played with that toy. But if you've got a clown phobia, feel free to skip this one!*

balloon

Start with both hands closed into fists in front of your mouth, and then open your hands as you move them outward to the sides of your face.

✳ Memory tip

It's like you're showing the balloon inflating.

◉ When to use the sign

When you have a little one who loves balloons, you realize they are everywhere! Sign **BALLOON** as you see them at the grocery store and other places around town.

◉ What to look for

Your little one might throw her arms wide open or make a blowing noise if you've paired a sound effect with this sign.

birthday

Bend the middle finger of your dominant hand and touch it to your chin and then your chest.

✳ Memory tip

The first step of this sign (when you tap your middle finger to your chin) is the sign for **FAVORITE** in ASL. It's like you're saying "It's my favorite day!"

◉ When to use the sign

Sign **BIRTHDAY** to talk about an upcoming or recent birthday celebration. On your child's birthday, you can point to him and say, "It's your **BIRTHDAY**—hooray!"

◉ What to look for

Your child might touch his face and body with his pointer finger or whole hand.

party

Make *P* handshapes (page 39) with both hands and swing them from side to side in unison.

✳ Memory tip
It's like people dancing together at a party.

🕐 When to use the sign
Sign **PARTY** any time you're bringing your little one to a family celebration or lively event with lots of friends and excitement.

👁 What to look for
Your child might wave both hands excitedly.

SIGNING FUN

Sign and Sing: *"Happy Birthday to You"*

Balloons and presents and cake—oh my! Is there anything more exciting for the toddler and preschool set than a birthday party? Little ones learn to sing along to this familiar tune early on, and by teaching them the signs, they can start even earlier! You can even stage a mock birthday celebration for a favorite stuffed animal to practice the song.

HAPPY BIRTHDAY to **YOU**

HAPPY BIRTHDAY to **YOU**

HAPPY BIRTHDAY dear [name]

HAPPY BIRTHDAY to **YOU**!

Key Vocabulary

HAPPY, p. 31

BIRTHDAY, p. 75

YOU, p. 102

Sign and Read: *Birthday Monsters!* by Sandra Boynton

With classic Boynton silliness, *Birthday Monsters!* tells the story of a group of monsters who show up to help a bewildered hippo celebrate his special day. As you can imagine, things go a little haywire (what did you expect from a bunch of monsters?), but fortunately, they make it all right in the end. With this book, in addition to signing along with the text, I like to use signs for the illustrations. For example, when the story starts, the hippo is sleeping in its **BED**. And when the monsters barge in, they're all wearing party hats and holding **BALLOONS**. Pick and choose from the signs provided to sign along to this story in the way that's most fun for you and your little one.

Key Vocabulary

BIRTHDAY, p. 75   **MONSTER,** p. 73   **BED,** p. 18

BALLOON, p. 75   **MORNING,** p. 52   **READY,** p. 47

WAIT, p. 135   **CAKE,** p. 64

Thoughts & Feelings

WHEN YOU FIRST start signing with your baby, it makes sense to start with physical things your baby can see, touch, and taste. Signs for things like **BALL** (page 22), **MILK** (page 16), and **DOG** (page 21) are great signs to start with—because they are tangible objects, it's easier for your baby to connect the spoken word to the visual sign.

But once your baby gets into the toddler and preschool age range, you'll be eager to expand her vocabulary beyond just items around the house in order to engage in more sophisticated communication.

In this chapter, you'll learn an incredible assortment of next-level signs to expand your signing repertoire. First, we'll start with signs for emotions so your little one can start to identify and label her feelings. You'll learn how to sign **CRY** (page 84), **FRUSTRATED** (page 87), and even two different ways to say "**I LOVE YOU**" (page 91).

You'll also learn signs for movements, like **JUMP** (page 94) and **DANCE** (page 95), to incorporate into conversation and physical games with your child, and two of my favorite songs for teaching action words.

Learning opposites is an important milestone for preschoolers, but you can get started early with sign language. In order for children to begin using descriptive words, like **BIG** (page 103) and **LITTLE** (page 103), they first need to understand these concepts. Signing is a fantastic way to introduce these words as you can literally show your child what they mean with your hands!

feelings

love

Bend the middle finger of your dominant hand and brush it upward on your chest in a circular motion.

✳ Memory tip

It's like you're indicating your heart and showing all the feelings you have inside.

☺ When to use the sign

Sign **FEELINGS** when your child is emotional and you're not sure what's going on. Ask, "What are you **FEELING** right now?" Use the other signs in this section to help your child express himself.

👁 What to look for

Your baby might tap or brush his chest or stomach with his whole hand.

Cross your arms over your chest and give a little squeeze.

✳ Memory tip

It's like you're giving yourself a hug.

☺ When to use the sign

You can sign **LOVE** to express your love for your child or to indicate that you are feeling loved by her. When your child is hugging her favorite blanket or stuffed toy, you can say, "Oh, you **LOVE** that so much!"

👁 What to look for

Your baby might press both hands or fists to her chest without crossing her arms.

laugh

Point to the corners of your mouth with both pointer fingers, and brush your fingers up and out a few times.

✳ Memory tip
It's like you're showing your smiling, laughing face.

🕐 When to use the sign
Sign **LAUGH** when you see something funny or see someone else cracking up. Pair this sign with silly laughing sounds ("ha, ha, ha!") to get your baby's attention and make it fun.

👁 What to look for
Your baby might make some funny laughing sounds himself to go along with this sign, which could get you both giggling.

❋ Similar signs
The sign for **LAUGH** is very similar to the sign for **SMILE**. To sign **SMILE**, point your fingers as in **LAUGH**, but just move your fingers up and out once, showing your big smile.

cry

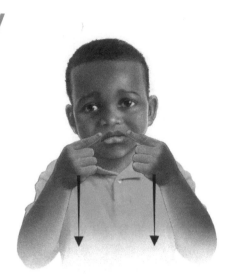

Touch your pointer fingers to your cheeks and slide them down your face. You can move your hands together or alternately.

✳ Memory tip
It's like you're showing the tears running down your cheeks.

🕐 When to use the sign
Sign **CRY** when your baby is sad as a way of acknowledging her feelings. Your facial expression should look sad or concerned to keep consistent with the meaning of the sign and to show compassion for how your baby is feeling. This will help her to know that you understand.

👁 What to look for
Toddlers usually get this one pretty accurately!

*Babies are naturally very empathetic. My daughters would sign **CRY** when they heard a baby crying in a store. It let me know they were concerned, and I could respond, "Yes, the baby is sad, but don't worry, his mommy will help him."*

silly

Hold your dominant hand in a *Y* handshape (page 40) in front of your nose and give it a little shake. Make a silly face to match!

✴ Memory tip
It's a silly sign to go with your silly face!

☺ When to use the sign
Sign **SILLY** when your little one is being a goofball or when something funny happens.

👁 What to look for
Your baby might wave or flap his whole hand or pointer finger near his face.

shy

Bend your dominant hand and place the backs of your fingers on your cheek, and then rotate your wrist forward.

✴ Memory tip
It's like you're trying to hide behind your hand because you're so shy.

☺ When to use the sign
This is a really helpful sign for little ones who are **SHY** around people they don't know well. If a friend or relative is being a little too friendly with your child, you can help the child out by labeling her feelings. "She's just feeling a little **SHY** right now." Once your little one learns this sign, she can let you know when she is feeling shy and might need some distance.

👁 What to look for
Your baby might wipe or brush her cheek with her hand.

excited

Bend the middle finger of both hands and brush them upward alternately and quickly on your chest in a circular motion.

✳ Memory tip
It's like the excitement is bubbling up and out of your chest.

☺ When to use the sign
Sign **EXCITED** when you've got something special going on and your little one is super happy about it. If your toddler is squealing with excitement about the playground as you park the car, you can say, "You are feeling so **EXCITED** to go on the swings!" as you unbuckle his car seat.

👁 What to look for
Your baby might pat or swipe at his chest with excitement.

scared

Start with your fists closed at your sides and "pop" them open in front of your chest.

✳ Memory tip
It's like you're showing the startled feeling inside when something scares you.

☺ When to use the sign
If your little one gets startled or scared, you can say, "Wow, those fireworks really **SCARED** you! It's okay, you're safe with Mommy." Make sure your facial expression matches the sign, and make big, scared eyes when you sign **SCARED**.

👁 What to look for
Baby will likely mimic your facial expressions and make a big jolt with her body and arms.

brave

Start with your open hands touching the front of your shoulders, and move them away from your body as you close your hands into fists.

✱ Memory tip

It's like you're showing your courage moving from your insides into your strong arms and hands.

☺ When to use the sign

Sign **BRAVE** when your child does something for the first time, like visiting the dentist or petting a dog. Say, "Wow, you were so **BRAVE** today when you got your teeth cleaned for the first time!"

👁 What to look for

When a child is old enough to understand the idea of being brave, he will likely be able to do this sign pretty accurately.

✿ Similar signs

The sign for **BRAVE** is the same as the sign for **HEALTHY**.

frustrated

Make a *B* handshape (page 38) with your dominant hand with your palm out, and then gently knock the back of your hand into your chin.

✱ Memory tip

It's like you're bumping into something that's in your way, which is very frustrating.

☺ When to use the sign

When your child is getting fussy because she can't make a puzzle piece fit or her toy is stuck, you can say, "You seem **FRUSTRATED**! Do you need some help?"

👁 What to look for

Your baby might pat her face with the palm of her hand.

SIGNING FUN

Sign and Sing: "If You're Happy and You Know It"

In this twist on the classic children's song, use your new sign language vocabulary to show how you're feeling! Feel free to exaggerate the signs to demonstrate the emotion behind each word and sign. Sign and say the feeling word together, and then continue doing the sign as you sing the sound effect that goes with the sign ("Ha ha!" and so on).

Key Vocabulary

LAUGH, p. 84   **CRY,** p. 84   **EXCITED,** p. 86

If you're happy and you know it then you **LAUGH** (Ha ha!)

If you're happy and you know it then you **LAUGH** (Ha ha!)

If you're happy and you know it then your face will surely show it

If you're happy and you know it then you **LAUGH** (Ha ha!).

If you're sad and you know it then you **CRY** (Boo hoo!)

If you're sad and you know it then you **CRY** (Boo hoo!)

If you're sad and you know it then your face will surely show it

If you're sad and you know it then you **CRY** (Boo hoo!).

If you're **EXCITED** and you know it go like this (Woo hoo!)

If you're **EXCITED** and you know it go like this (Woo hoo!)

If you're **EXCITED** and you know it then your face will surely show it

If you're **EXCITED** and you know it go like this (Woo hoo!).

Sign and Read: *How Does Baby Feel?* by Karen Katz

This sweet and simple lift-the-flap board book is an easy way to introduce feeling signs to babies and young toddlers. The book shows a number of familiar scenarios and asks the reader to guess how the baby in the book is feeling. Give your toddler a chance to guess what the baby in the story is feeling before reading the answer under each flap, and you can introduce the sign for that feeling.

Key Vocabulary

HUNGRY, p. 57

HAPPY, p. 31

SLEEP, p. 51

SILLY, p. 85

LOVE, p. 83

Sign and Read: *The Way I Feel*
by Janan Cain

This beautifully illustrated picture book is great for preschool-age and older children to learn to identify and label more complex emotions. The artwork and text do a wonderful job of illustrating the feelings of each new emotion and offer lots of opportunity for discussion about our complex feelings.

Key Vocabulary

SILLY, p. 85

SCARED, p. 86

HAPPY, p. 31

CRY, p. 84

FRUSTRATED, p. 87

SHY, p. 85

EXCITED, p. 86

FEELINGS, p. 83

Advanced Signing: How to say "I love you" in ASL

Expressing love and affection for babies is something parents do right from the start. But it's a really special moment when your baby is able to clearly communicate that they love you, too! There are two ways to sign **I LOVE YOU** in ASL. You can do each of the signs **ME** (which is also **I**), **LOVE**, and **YOU**, or you can do the I-L-Y sign, also seen on page 28, which is a combination of the first letters of the three words *I love you*.

Key Vocabulary

ME, p. 102   **LOVE,** p. 83   **YOU,** p. 102

I LOVE YOU, p. 28

movement

stand

Make a *V* handshape (page 39) with your dominant hand and place it upside down on the palm of your opposite hand.

✳ Memory tip
It's like your fingers are the legs and your supporting hand is the ground.

◷ When to use the sign
Sign **STAND** when playing games or giving directions to your little one.

◉ What to look for
Your child might touch his pointer finger to his palm.

✿ Similar signs
As you will see from the other signs in this section, the sign for **STAND** is the foundation for a number of movement signs, including **FALL DOWN** (page 94), **JUMP** (page 94), and **DANCE** (page 95).

sit

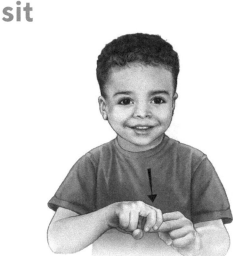

Make a *U* handshape (page 39) with your nondominant hand and hold it parallel to the floor with your palm facing down. Make a bent *U* handshape with your dominant hand and place your bent fingers on the opposite fingers.

✳ Memory tip
It's like your supporting hand is a bench and your dominant hand is legs sitting down.

◷ When to use the sign
SIT is a very useful sign for toddlers, who often need reminding to sit down at the table or in the shopping cart. You'll even be able to give a silent reminder to **SIT** down from across the room.

◉ What to look for
Your baby might sign **SIT** by placing her hand on her opposite hand or arm.

✿ Similar signs
To sign **SWING**, sign **SIT** and then swing your "sitting" fingers back and forth.

fall down

Start with the fingers of your dominant hand in an inverted *V* handshape (page 39) on your opposite palm (see the sign for **STAND**, page 93), then move the wrist of your dominant hand to the side and down.

✳ Memory tip
It's like your fingers are your legs and you're falling over.

◎ When to use the sign
Use this sign to talk about something you saw or something that happened during your day. "Remember when you were **JUMPING** (page 94) in the bounce house and then you **FELL DOWN**? That was so **SILLY** (page 85)!" (Note: Action words can be used in past tense, as in this example.)

◉ What to look for
Your baby might do this sign with just his pointer finger or with all of his fingers touching his palm.

jump

Start with the fingers of your dominant hand in an inverted *V* handshape (page 39) on your opposite palm (see the sign for **STAND**, page 93), then bend your fingers and lift your dominant hand two times.

✳ Memory tip
It's like your fingers are legs jumping up from the ground.

◎ When to use the sign
Sign **JUMP** when doing a jumping activity, such as in a small bouncy house for toddlers or a trampoline park for older kids.

◉ What to look for
Little ones will likely "jump" their whole hand instead of just two fingers.

dance

Start with the fingers of your dominant hand in an inverted *V* handshape (page 39) on your opposite palm (see the sign for **STAND**, page 93), then swing your dominant hand side to side a little bit.

✳ Memory tip
It's like your fingers are legs moving gracefully over the dance floor.

☺ When to use the sign
Make this sign into a fun freeze-dance game with your little one. Sign **DANCE** to let her know it's time to dance, and sign **STOP** (page 104) when it's time to freeze. You can even play this without music, which can be a handy game in situations like when you're stuck waiting in line.

👁 What to look for
Your baby might swing her whole arm from side to side.

walk

Hold both of your flat hands in front of your body with palms facing down, then move your hands up and down alternately.

✳ Memory tip
It's like your hands are feet walking down the street.

☺ When to use the sign
Sign **WALK** to remind your running toddler to slow down his pace!

👁 What to look for
Your little one might wave his hands together instead of alternately.

run

Make *L* handshapes (page 38) with both hands with your pointer fingers slightly bent. With palms facing each other, hook the pointer of your dominant hand around the thumb of your nondominant hand, and bounce your hands together up and down as you move them slightly away from your body.

✳ Memory tip
Think of your hands as runners in a close race.

🕐 When to use the sign
You can play a walking and running game that is similar to Simon Says or Red Light, Green Light. Rotate through the signs for **WALK** (page 95), **STOP** (page 104), and **RUN**, and see who gets to the finish line first!

👁 What to look for
This is a pretty tricky sign, even for grown-ups! Look for little ones clasping their hands together and moving them quickly up and down.

swim

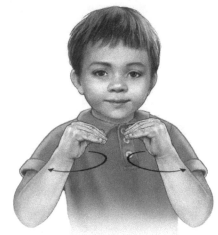

Hold your bent hands in front of your chest and move them away from your body and to your sides, either one or two times.

✳ Memory tip
It's just like you're swimming the breast stroke.

🕐 When to use the sign
If your little one takes swim lessons or you're going to the beach, you can use this sign to talk about going **SWIMMING** or how much fun it is to **SWIM**.

👁 What to look for
Your baby might flap her arms and look more like she's flying than swimming.

SIGNING FUN

Sign and Sing: "This Is the Way"

Many of the movement signs you learned in this section look like the motion they represent. This simple song demonstrates the signs in a fun and interactive way while also acknowledging that what you're doing with your hands is sign language! You can use any of the movement signs from this section, but I'll start you off with my three favorites: **DANCE**, **JUMP**, and **WALK**.

Key Vocabulary

DANCE, p. 95   **JUMP,** p. 94   **WALK,** p. 95

(Sung to the tune of "Here We Go 'Round the Mulberry Bush")

This is the way we move our hands, move our hands, move our hands [sign **DANCE**]

This is the way we move our hands, when we're signing **DANCING**.

This is the way we move our hands, move our hands, move our hands [sign **JUMP**]

This is the way we move our hands, when we're signing **JUMPING**.

This is the way we move our hands, move our hands, move our hands [sign **WALK**]

This is the way we move our hands, when we're signing **WALKING**.

Sign and Read: *Barnyard Dance!* by Sandra Boynton

This short board book is quintessential Boynton. What could be more fun and silly than a bunch of farm animals having a hoedown? But what I really love about this book is that it provides an awesome opportunity to build vocabulary. You can pair the movement signs you've learned in this section with new, more sophisticated ones to expand your child's vocabulary even further. For example, use *prance* with the sign for **DANCE**. You can also use *promenade* and *strut* with the sign for **WALK**, *bounce* with the sign for **JUMP**, and *skitter* with the sign for **RUN**. Of course, it's also a great opportunity to practice your animal signs, too!

Key Vocabulary

DANCE, p. 95   **JUMP,** p. 94   **WALK,** p. 95

STAND, p. 93   **DOG,** p. 21   **SHEEP,** p. 35

ALL DONE, p. 18

opposites

yes

Make an *S* handshape (page 39) with your dominant hand in front of your shoulder, and bend your wrist up and down a few times.

✳ Memory tip
It's like your fist is your head nodding "yes!"

◎ When to use the sign
If your toddler signs **GRAPE** (page 59) to you, you can sign and say, "**YES**, let's get you some **GRAPES**! You must be **HUNGRY** (page 57)!"

👁 What to look for
It might look like your baby is waving hello or bye-bye.

My daughter would sign **YES** *while also nodding her head up and down. It was super cute!*

no

Hold your dominant hand in front of your shoulder, and open and close your pointer and middle fingers to your thumb a few times.

✳ Memory tip
This is a simplified version of fingerspelling *N–O*.

◎ When to use the sign
Use your voice and sign language to convey the tone of this sign. Sign **NO** quickly and say "No, no, no" gently to your child, or bring your fingers to your thumb once with more force and a louder spoken "No!" to really make your point!

👁 What to look for
Your baby might open and close his whole hand.

✿ Similar signs
If you do this handshape and motion in front of your mouth, that's the sign for **DUCK**.

up

Extend the pointer finger of your dominant hand and move it toward the sky.

✳ **Memory tip**
Point **UP**—it couldn't be simpler!

☺ **When to use the sign**
When your baby is reaching up, wanting to be picked up, you can ask, "Do you want to go **UP**?"

👁 **What to look for**
Your child might do this with her whole hand early on.

down

Extend the pointer finger of your dominant hand and move it toward the ground.

✳ **Memory tip**
Point **DOWN**—easy peasy!

☺ **When to use the sign**
When you're holding your little one and he starts to wiggle, you can ask, "Do you want to get **DOWN**?" You can use this as an alternative to **ALL DONE** (page 18) after your child has mastered that sign.

👁 **What to look for**
Your child might point at the ground or swing his arm downward.

me

Touch the pointer finger of your dominant hand to your chest.

✱ **Memory tip**
It's like you're pointing to yourself.

◷ **When to use the sign**
When playing with your little one, point to yourself to indicate that it's your turn or to pass something to you. You can say something like, "It's my turn; can you give **ME** the ball?"

◉ **What to look for**
Your baby might touch her finger, fist, or whole hand to her chest.

✿ **Similar signs**
You can use this sign for either ME or I (for example, "It's my turn, can **I** have the ball?"). If you place your open, flat hand on your chest, that is the sign for **MINE**.

you

Extend the pointer of your dominant hand and point it away from your body.

✱ **Memory tip**
It's like you're pointing at someone who is facing you.

◷ **When to use the sign**
Sign **YOU** to let your baby know something is for him. If he offers you a bite of his half-eaten snack, you can say, "Thank you. **YOU** eat it! That's your snack."

◉ **What to look for**
Babies usually get this one right!

✿ **Similar signs**
Hold your open hand out, fingers pointing up and palm facing out, to sign **YOUR**.

big

Hold your open, flat hands in front of your body with palms facing each other, and spread them outward and away from each other.

✳ Memory tip

It's like you're showing how large an item is.

◷ When to use the sign

Sign **BIG** when you are reading a book with something **BIG** in it or when you see a **BIG** elephant or dump truck. You can use this sign when reading the book *The Little Mouse, the Red Ripe Strawberry, and the Big Hungry Bear* (see page 66).

◉ What to look for

Your baby might exaggerate this sign by throwing his arms wide open, and that's just fine—very effective communication, actually!

little

Hold your open, flat hands in front of your body with palms facing each other, and move them inward and closer to each other.

✳ Memory tip

It's like you're showing how small something is.

◷ When to use the sign

You can use this sign with the words **SMALL**, **LITTLE**, and even **TINY**. Point out the **LITTLE PEAS** (page 61) on your child's plate or the **LITTLE CATERPILLAR** (page 172) crawling on a leaf. Use it when you read *Goodnight Moon* (page 54) and talk about the **LITTLE** mouse.

◉ What to look for

Your baby will likely bring his hands together (like a clap), as it's pretty hard to stop before your hands touch when you're little.

stop

Hold your nondominant hand open in front of your body with the palm facing up, and bring the outside edge of your dominant hand down onto your open palm in a chopping motion.

✳ Memory tip
It's like you're dropping a gate to stop something from going forward.

☺ When to use the sign
Sign **STOP** to let your toddler know to stop and wait for you. Use a serious tone of voice if you want your child to know it's important to pay attention when you use this sign.

👁 What to look for
Toddlers and preschoolers can do a pretty good karate-style chop to demonstrate this sign!

*I used this as a safety sign with my daughters instead of the sign for **NO** (page 100). I would use it only for serious warnings, like not to touch an electrical outlet.*

go

Start with both hands near your chest with pointer fingers extended and pointing up, then swing your hands downward so both pointers are pointing away from you.

✳ Memory tip
It's like you're pointing in the direction you want to go.

☺ When to use the sign
Sign **GO** when giving your child directions. You can say, "**GO** over there and get the **BALL** (page 22)." You can also use this sign along with **STOP** to play a stop-and-go movement game!

👁 What to look for
Kids often get this one right and do it with enthusiasm!

*My younger daughter loved this sign as a toddler and made a game out of it. She would sign and say "**GO!**" and then run into the other room, and then do the same coming back. It was pretty funny!*

open

Start with both hands in *B* handshapes (page 38) in front of your body, touching with palms facing down, then lift them up and outward so your palms are facing each other.

✳ Memory tip
It's like the flaps of a cardboard box opening.

☺ When to use the sign
Sign **OPEN** when playing with your toddler. Hide a toy in a shoebox and ask him to **OPEN** it. Then talk about what he found inside. You can open anything together and make it fun: closets, cabinets, boxes, packages, cards—you name it.

👁 What to look for
Your baby might throw his arms open wide.

❋ Similar signs
OPEN can also be signed with the palms facing away from your body, which looks more like opening doors.

closed

Start with both hands in *B* handshapes (page 38) in front of your body with palms facing each other, and then move them inward and down so they end up touching with palms down.

✳ Memory tip
It's like the flaps of a cardboard box closing.

☺ When to use the sign
Sign **CLOSE** to ask your child to close a door or drawer. You can also use this sign to explain that a store or restaurant is **CLOSED**.

👁 What to look for
It might look like one big clap.

in

Make a C handshape (page 38) with your nondominant hand with the palm facing sideways. With all the fingertips of your dominant hand touching, move your dominant hand down into the open C of your opposite hand.

✻ Memory tip
It's like you're putting something in a cup.

◷ When to use the sign
Sign **IN** when playing with toys or cleaning up. Take a small bucket and ask your little one to put all the blocks **IN** the bucket.

◉ What to look for
Your baby might clasp his hands together.

out

Start with all the fingers of your dominant hand tucked inside your nondominant hand, which is held in a C handshape (page 38) with the palm facing sideways. Lift your dominant hand out and away from your nondominant hand.

✻ Memory tip
It's like you're taking something out of a cup.

◷ When to use the sign
Practice the signs for **IN** and **OUT** by saying and signing the words while placing toys or food in and out of containers.

◉ What to look for
Your baby might clasp her hands together and then throw them wide open.

same

Make a *Y* handshape (page 40) with your dominant hand, palm facing down, and then move it from side to side a few times.

✳ Memory tip
It's like you're pointing to two identical things at the same time.

☺ When to use the sign
Place two items together (like two strawberries) and say and sign **SAME**. You can say something like, "These two **STRAWBERRIES** (page 59) are the **SAME**. They are both **RED** (page 155)."

👁 What to look for
Your baby might swing his pointer finger or whole hand from side to side.

different

Start with your pointer fingers crossed in front of your body, and move them up and away from each other.

✳ Memory tip
It's like you're showing the difference by moving your fingers in opposite directions.

☺ When to use the sign
Place two items together (like two different-colored grapes) and say and sign **DIFFERENT**. You can say something like, "These two **GRAPES** (page 59) are **DIFFERENT**. This one is **PURPLE** (page 158) and this one is **GREEN** (page 157)."

👁 What to look for
Your baby might touch her pointer fingers or her whole hands together and then move them apart.

wet

Start with both hands in front of your chest with palms up and fingers open and relaxed, then lower both hands as you close your fingers to your thumbs.

✳ Memory tip
It's like you're showing water dripping off of something that is soaking wet.

☺ When to use the sign
Sign **WET** to describe the **DOG** (page 21) after his **BATH** (page 19) or your little one's hair after **SWIMMING** (page 96).

👁 What to look for
It might look like your baby is waving with both hands.

dry

Hold your dominant hand in front of your chin with your pointer finger extended, then slide it toward your dominant side as your bend your pointer finger.

✳ Memory tip
It's like you're wiping your chin dry.

☺ When to use the sign
Sign and say, "Let's get you nice and **DRY**!" as you dry your baby after a bath.

👁 What to look for
Your baby might wipe his chin or cheek with his whole hand.

good

Touch the fingertips of your flat dominant hand to your chin and move your hand down and away from your face, and then stop your moving hand with the palm of your opposite hand.

✳ Memory tip
It's like you tasted something delicious and want to keep it.

◎ When to use the sign
This sign pairs well with other signs you'll find in this book, including **MORNING** (page 52) and **NIGHT** (page 53).

👁 What to look for
It might look like your baby is blowing kisses and/or clapping her hands.

✳ Similar signs
This sign is very similar to the sign for **THANK YOU**, which is done with just the dominant-hand portion of the sign.

bad

Touch the fingertips of your flat dominant hand to your chin and move your hand away from your face, twisting your hand so your palm is facing away from you.

✳ Memory tip
It's like you tasted something yucky and want to push it away.

◎ When to use the sign
You can use this sign to describe behavior ("The **DOG** [page 21] chewed daddy's shoe; he was being a **BAD DOG**.") or something your child doesn't like ("Does that taste **BAD**?").

👁 What to look for
Your child might start this sign with his palm facing away from his chin.

SIGNING FUN

Sign and Sing: "The Noble Duke of York"

It's fun to gently bounce your little one on your knees while singing a simple song or chant. "*The Noble Duke of York*" is a great way to teach the difference between **UP** and **DOWN**, because your baby goes up and down on your knees as you sing the song. To do this song as a lap bounce, sit on the floor with your legs extended and sit your baby on your knees facing you. Support your baby under his arms and lift your knees up and down along with the lyrics of the song. Once your little one has learned the meaning of the words from the lap bounce, you can sing and sign it anytime you want. With toddlers and preschoolers, you can stand and do the signs as you bend and straighten your back to go **DOWN** and **UP**.

Key Vocabulary

UP, p. 101   **DOWN,** p. 101   **SILLY,** p. 85

(Sung to the tune of "*A-Hunting We Will Go*")

Oh, the Noble Duke of York [gently bouncing knees]

He had ten thousand men

He marched them **UP** to the top of the hill [lift knees up]

And marched them **DOWN** again. [lower knees down]

And when they're **UP**, they're **UP** [lift knees up]

And when they're **DOWN**, they're **DOWN** [lower knees down]

And when they're only halfway **UP** [lift knees up halfway]

They're neither **UP** nor **DOWN**. [lift knees up then drop them down]

He marched them to the left [bounce and tilt baby to the left]

He marched them to the right [bounce and tilt baby to the right]

He even marched them upside down [gently turn baby upside down if able]

Oh what a **SILLY** sight!

Sign and Play: "Roly Poly"

"Roly Poly" is a staple in many library story times and preschool classrooms. It's a simple chant that teaches opposites in a simple and clear way. It's a great way to teach opposite signs, too! When I do this song, I do the sign in slow motion to give the children a chance to really take it in. For example, when signing **UP** with these lyrics, start the sign with the first *up* and finish the sign by the third *up*. Little ones love to sign along with this one as the pace is just right for little hands to keep up!

Key Vocabulary

UP, p. 101

DOWN, p. 101

IN, p. 106

OUT, p. 106

OPEN, p. 105

CLOSE, p. 105

Roly Poly, Roly Poly

UP, UP, UP

Roly Poly, Roly Poly

DOWN, DOWN, DOWN

Roly Poly, Roly Poly

IN, IN, IN

Roly Poly, Roly Poly

OUT, OUT, OUT

Roly Poly, Roly Poly

OPEN, OPEN, OPEN

Roly Poly, Roly Poly

CLOSE, CLOSE, CLOSE

5

Around Town

WHEN YOU FIRST introduce sign language to your little one, it's ideal to begin by working with familiar items that are close at hand at home, like **CAT** (page 21) or **BOOK** (page 22). But as your baby grows and develops, her world and vocabulary will grow and expand, too.

In this chapter, you'll start by learning signs for **HOME** (page 115) and **FAMILY** (page 118). You'll also learn signs for common things found around your home, like **DOOR** (page 116) and **CHAIR** (page 117), as well as the signs for important people in your baby's life, like **AUNT** (page 118), **COUSIN** (pages 119 and 120), and **BABYSITTER** (page 120).

As your baby grows into a toddler and beyond, she'll become increasingly interested in your routines and the typical places you visit. This is a great time to introduce new signs for places, like the **LIBRARY** (page 126), **STORE** (page 126), and **SCHOOL** (page 142).

As she grows and gains increasing independence, your little one will learn new skills to stay healthy and safe. In this chapter, you'll learn some important signs to help you guide your toddler and preschooler to be **CAREFUL** (page 134), to **WAIT** (page 135), and to always remember to **WASH HANDS** (page 137) so she doesn't get **SICK** (page 137).

Lastly, if your little one attends day care or preschool, you know that **SCHOOL** (page 142) becomes an important extended community to children. Have fun helping your child learn the signs for familiar items, like **BACKPACK** (page 143), **PAPER** (page 145), and **SCISSORS** (page 146). At the end of each section, you'll also find fun and easy books and songs to practice these new signs. Have fun!

home and family

home

With your dominant hand, bring all your fingers together and touch your face near your mouth and then your cheekbone.

✳ Memory tip
This is a modified blend of the signs for **EAT** (page 16) and **BED** (page 18), because home is where you eat and sleep.

☺ When to use the sign
When you're heading home after running errands, say to your child, "It's time to go **HOME** now." When you arrive at your home, sign and say, "We're **HOME**!"

👁 What to look for
Your baby might touch his face twice in the same spot.

house

With flat hands, touch your fingertips together so they are making an upside-down *V* shape, and move your hands down and away from each other slightly, then drop your wrists so your fingers are pointing up.

✳ Memory tip
It's like you're showing the shape of a house.

☺ When to use the sign
You can sign **HOUSE** to talk about the houses in your neighborhood, a doghouse, a kid-sized playhouse, and even a little dollhouse. When reading *Goodnight Moon* (page 54), sign **HOUSE** when you point out the "little toy house."

👁 What to look for
Your baby might move her hands far apart and then down.

door

Start with two *B* handshapes (page 38) touching with palms facing forward, then pull your dominant hand toward you and to the side so your palm is facing sideways, twice quickly.

✳ Memory tip

It's like a door opening and closing.

◎ When to use the sign

You can practice signing **DOOR** when your little one is playing with the kitchen cabinet doors. You can say, "Are you opening the **DOOR**? What's inside?" You can also sign **DOOR** when you sing the song "Miss Polly Had a Dolly" (see page 139).

◉ What to look for

Your little one might do this with a much larger or smaller motion than you, depending on his developmental ability.

window

Stack your flat hands in front of your chest with palms toward you, and then lift your top hand twice.

✳ Memory tip

It's like a window sliding open.

◎ When to use the sign

When you see something out the window, you can say, "Look out the **WINDOW**! Do you see the **SQUIRREL** (page 169)?"

◉ What to look for

Your child might do this sign with her palms facing down instead of toward her, or she might lift both hands together.

chair

Make a *U* handshape (page 39) with your nondominant hand and hold it parallel to the floor with the palm facing down. Make a bent *U* handshape with your dominant hand and tap your bent fingers on the opposite fingers two times.

✳ Memory tip

It's like your supporting hand is a chair and your dominant hand is the pair of legs sitting down.

◷ When to use the sign

Sign **CHAIR** when it's time to get seated at the table for a meal. You can say, "Please sit down in your **CHAIR**; it's time to **EAT** (page 16)."

◉ What to look for

Your baby might sign **CHAIR** by placing his hand on his opposite hand or arm.

✿ Similar signs

CHAIR and **SIT** are very similar signs. See Noun/Verb Pairs in ASL (page 123) for more information.

table

Hold both arms in front of your body with flat hands and palms facing down, and bring your arms together twice.

✳ Memory tip

It's like you're patting the flat surface of a tabletop.

◷ When to use the sign

Sign **TABLE** when you are using a table for meals or as a place to **DRAW** (page 145) or do a **PUZZLE** (page 71).

◉ What to look for

Your baby might do an exaggerated clapping motion.

✿ Similar signs

This is also the sign for **DESK**.

family

Start with two *F* handshapes (page 38) touching with palms facing out, then twist your hands so your palms are facing you and your pinky fingers are touching.

✻ **Memory tip**
It's like a family circle.

◉ **When to use the sign**
Sign **FAMILY** when you are going to a family get-together for a visit or special occasion.

◉ **What to look for**
This is a pretty sophisticated sign, so younger toddlers might try to do it with a rough approximation, such as with just their pointer fingers.

❋ **Similar signs**
There are a number of signs done with this same motion, but different letter shapes change the meaning. If you do it with *C* handshapes (page 38), it means **CLASS** (page 142). If you do it with *T* handshapes (page 39), it means **TEAM**.

aunt

Make an *A* handshape (page 38) with your dominant hand and circle it near your jaw.

✻ **Memory tip**
A is for *aunt* (see Male and Female Signs, page 122).

◉ **When to use the sign**
Pair this sign with the name of a favorite aunt, or use it for all of your child's aunties. You can pair it with whatever language you use for aunts in your family (auntie, *tia*, etc.).

◉ **What to look for**
Your child might shake or wave her fist.

uncle

Make an *U* handshape (page 39) with your dominant hand and circle it near your temple.

✱ **Memory tip**
U is for *uncle* (see Male and Female Signs, page 122).

◎ **When to use the sign**
Pair this sign with the name of a favorite uncle, or use it for all of your child's uncles. You can pair it with whatever language you use for uncles in your family (uncle, *tio*, etc.).

◉ **What to look for**
Your child might do this sign with his whole hand or just his pointer finger.

cousin (female)

Make a *C* handshape (page 38) with your dominant hand and twist it near your chin.

✱ **Memory tip**
C is for *cousin* and it's signed near the chin for a female cousin (see Male and Female Signs, page 122).

◎ **When to use the sign**
If your child has one female cousin she spends a lot of time with, you can pair this sign with that cousin's first name.

◉ **What to look for**
Your baby might do this with an open hand or closed fist.

cousin (male)

Make a C handshape (page 38) with your dominant hand and twist it near your temple.

✳ Memory tip

C is for *cousin* and it's signed near the forehead for a male cousin (see Male and Female Signs, page 122).

☺ When to use the sign

If your child has one male cousin he spends a lot of time with, you can pair this sign with that cousin's first name.

👁 What to look for

Your baby might do this with an open hand or closed fist.

babysitter

Make two *K* handshapes (page 38) and stack them with your dominant hand on top, then circle them together away from your body twice.

✳ Memory tip

K stands for *keep*, as your babysitter keeps your little one safe.

☺ When to use the sign

Sign **BABYSITTER** when the babysitter or nanny is coming. If you have someone who comes regularly, you can pair this sign with the babysitter's name.

👁 What to look for

Your baby might clasp her hands together and shake or wiggle them.

girl

Make a fist with your dominant hand and drag your thumb along your jawline from ear to chin.

✱ Memory tip
It's like you're showing where the ribbon of an old-fashioned bonnet would be.

◎ When to use the sign
Sign **GIRL** for any young female characters in books you read with your child.

👁 What to look for
Your child might swipe his pointer finger along his cheek.

boy

Open and close your fingers to your thumb in front of your forehead a few times.

✱ Memory tip
It's like you're grabbing the brim of your baseball cap.

◎ When to use the sign
Sign **BOY** for any young male characters in books you read with your child.

👁 What to look for
Your little one might wave near her face or open and close her hand in another location.

SIGNING FUN

Advanced Signing: Male and Female Signs

In ASL, all female signs are done on the lower half of the face, usually near the chin or jawline. Male signs are done on the upper half of the face, usually near the temple or forehead. For example, **MOM**, **GRANDMOTHER**, and **AUNT** are all done near or around the chin. Similarly, **DAD**, **GRANDFATHER**, and **UNCLE** are all done near or around the forehead. The reason for this convention relates to the ASL signs for **BOY** and **GIRL**. **BOY** is signed at the forehead to represent a boy's cap, and **GIRL** is signed along the jawline to represent the ribbon of a bonnet. All of the other gender-related signs follow this fundamental rule.

As awareness spreads about more inclusive language, some signs are being done in a more gender-neutral way. For example, **COUSIN** can be signed at ear level, as opposed to by the forehead (male cousin) or jawline (female cousin). Also, as an alternative to **MOM** or **DAD**, you could also use the sign for **PARENT**, which is done by touching the thumb of your open hand first to your chin and then your forehead, which is a combination of the two signs.

Key Vocabulary

BOY, p. 121 **GIRL,** p. 121 **UNCLE,** p. 119

AUNT, p. 118 **MOM,** p. 26 **DAD,** p. 27

Advanced Signing: Noun/Verb Pairs in ASL

In ASL, the signs for certain words are very similar. The difference between them is just in the motion. These are called noun/verb pairs, and in these instances, the noun has two quick movements (see **CHAIR**, page 117), and the verb has one stronger movement (see **SIT**, page 93). Other examples of noun/verb pairs are **SCISSORS** (page 146) and **CUT**, and **CAR** (page 23) and **DRIVE**, to name a few.

Key Vocabulary

SIT, p. 93   **CHAIR,** p. 117   **SCISSORS,** p. 146

CAR, p. 23

my community

police officer

Make a C handshape (page 38) with your dominant hand, cross your arm over your body, and place your C hand on your chest. If you are right-handed, the C hand will be over your heart. However, if your left hand is dominant, the C hand will be on the opposite side of your chest.

✳ **Memory tip**
Remember C for *cop*, and you're showing where the police officer's badge goes.

☺ **When to use the sign**
Sign **POLICE** when you see an officer in the community or when you see or hear a police car.

👁 **What to look for**
Your child might do this with his fist and in the middle of his chest.

firefighter

Make a B handshape (page 38) with your dominant hand and hold it to your forehead with your palm facing out.

✳ **Memory tip**
It's like you're showing the shield on a firefighter's helmet.

☺ **When to use the sign**
Sign **FIREFIGHTER** when you see a firefighter in your community or when you see or hear a fire engine.

👁 **What to look for**
Your child might touch the palm of her hand to her forehead or face.

library

Make an *L* handshape (page 38) with your dominant hand and circle it in the space in front of your shoulder.

✱ Memory tip

L is for *library*.

☺ When to use the sign

Sign **LIBRARY** when you're going to the library to pick out some books. Show your little one the sign for **BOOK** (page 22) while you are there.

👁 What to look for

Your baby might wave his pointer finger in the air.

store

Start with both hands in front of your body, with all the fingertips of each hand touching and wrists bent so your fingers are pointing downward, then quickly swing both hands up and away from your body twice.

✱ Memory tip

It's like a salesperson handing you your bags after you make a purchase.

☺ When to use the sign

Sign **STORE** when you are heading to the grocery store or any retail location with your child. And once you're at the store, be sure to sign all the items you know—from **BALLOONS** (page 75) to **BERRIES** (page 59)!

👁 What to look for

Your baby might wave his fists downward.

church

Make a fist with your nondominant hand with your palm facing down, and make a C handshape (page 38) with your dominant hand and touch it to the back of your opposite hand twice.

✳ Memory tip
C is for church, with the sign representing the building sitting on the ground.

☺ When to use the sign
Sign **CHURCH** when visiting or passing a church of any denomination.

👁 What to look for
Your baby might clap her fists together.

❇ Similar signs
SYNAGOGUE is signed similarly but with the dominant hand in an S handshape (page 39) and the nondominant hand flat with palm facing down. **MOSQUE** is fingerspelled.

farm

With your dominant hand open, touch your thumb to the opposite side of your jaw and drag your thumb along your jawline, finishing on the dominant side.

✳ Memory tip
Think of a farmer wiping the sweat from his neck after a long day's work.

☺ When to use the sign
Sign **FARM** when passing or visiting a local farm or reading a book about a farm, like Big Red Barn by Margaret Wise Brown.

👁 What to look for
Your baby might wipe his chin or cheek.

❇ Similar signs
You can combine the sign for **FARM** with the sign for **HOUSE** (page 115)—**FARM-HOUSE**—to sign **BARN**.

work

Make *S* handshapes (page 39) with both hands, palms facing down, and knock your dominant hand on the back of your opposite hand twice.

✳ Memory tip
Think of stacking heavy rocks or banging something with a heavy hammer.

☺ When to use the sign
When dropping your child off at day care or when leaving the house for work, tell your child, "It's time for me to go to **WORK**, but I'll be back!" You can also combine this sign with **GOOD** (page 109) to say "Good job!" to your little one.

👁 What to look for
Your baby might clap with her hands open or with closed fists.

truck

Make *A* handshapes (page 38) with both hands and hold them in front of your waist with palms facing each other, and move them back and forth away from your body alternately.

✳ Memory tip
It's like you're driving a big truck.

☺ When to use the sign
Sign **TRUCK** when you see a large truck, like a dump truck, garbage truck, or big tractor trailer.

👁 What to look for
Your baby might move his hands alternately or together.

✻ Similar signs
TRUCK is similar to the sign for **CAR** (page 23) but with the hands a little lower and with a bigger motion.

helicopter

Make a 3 handshape (page 40) with your nondominant hand with the palm facing you, then place the palm of your open dominant hand on the opposite thumb and shake it slightly.

✳ Memory tip
Your top hand represents the helicopter's blades.

☺ When to use the sign
Sign **HELICOPTER** when you hear one outside or see one in a book.

👁 What to look for
Babies often place their palm on their opposite pointer finger.

boat

Curve both hands and hold them together with palms up, then bounce them gently away from you twice.

✳ Memory tip
Your hands are like a boat floating on water.

☺ When to use the sign
Sign **BOAT** when you see one, when playing with a toy boat in the bathtub, or when singing "Row, Row, Row Your Boat" (see page 131).

👁 What to look for
Your baby might clasp her hands together and shake them.

motorcycle

Make *S* handshapes (page 39) with both hands and hold them in front of you with palms facing down, then bend the wrist of your dominant hand twice.

✳ **Memory tip**

It's like you are gripping a motorcycle's handlebars and revving the engine.

☺ **When to use the sign**

Sign **MOTORCYLE** when you see a noisy motorcycle out on the street.

👁 **What to look for**

Your baby might bend one or both wrists at the same time.

SIGNING FUN

Sign and Sing: "Row, Row, Row Your Boat"

"Row, Row, Row Your Boat" is a simple and fun song to sign and sing with your little one. There are only three signs to learn: **BOAT**, gentle, **STREAM**, and **HAPPY**. It's fun to sing and sign this song when playing with a toy boat in the bathtub!

Key Vocabulary

BOAT, p. 129

STREAM, p. 180

HAPPY, p. 31

Row, row, row your **BOAT**

Gently down the **STREAM**

MERRILY, MERRILY, MERRILY, MERRILY [sign **HAPPY**]

Life is but a dream.

Advanced Signing: Signs for Jobs in ASL

In ASL, there are two different ways to sign for specific professions. For example, some professions, like **DOCTOR** (page 138), **POLICE OFFICER** (page 125), and **FIREFIGHTER** (page 125), have their own unique sign.

However, many professions are identified by adding the sign for **PERSON** to the primary activity of that career. When used in this capacity, the **PERSON** sign is referred to as the **AGENT**, which means "a person who does something."

You can learn the sign for **PERSON/AGENT** via the sign for **TEACHER** (page 143), which you can see has two steps to the sign. The first step (hands moving away from the forehead) is the sign for **TEACH**. The second half of this sign (flat hands with palms facing each other moving straight down at your sides) is the sign for **PERSON/AGENT**. **TEACH + PERSON/AGENT** is the sign for **TEACHER**.

In the following examples, adding the **PERSON/AGENT** sign (flat hands with palms facing each other moving straight down at your sides) gives you the sign for the profession:

LIBRARY (page 126) **+ PERSON/AGENT = LIBRARIAN**

MEDICINE (page 138) **+ PERSON/AGENT = PHARMACIST**

FARM (page 127) **+ PERSON/AGENT = FARMER**

STORE (page 126) **+ PERSON/AGENT = SALESPERSON**

WRITE (page 144) **+ PERSON/AGENT = WRITER**

DRAW (page 145) **+ PERSON/AGENT = ARTIST**

Key Vocabulary

TEACHER, p. 143   **LIBRARY,** p. 126   **MEDICINE,** p. 138

FARM, p. 127   **STORE,** p. 126   **WRITE,** p. 144

DRAW, p. 145

healthy and safe

careful

Make *K* handshapes (page 38) with both
hands, and hold your dominant hand
above the other hand with palms facing in
opposite directions. Lower and raise your
dominant hand so that your hands "knock"
together twice.

✳ Memory tip
It's like your hands are bumping into each other as a
warning to be careful.

☺ When to use the sign
Sign **CAREFUL** if your child is doing something that
might be dangerous if he isn't careful.

👁 What to look for
Your baby might touch his pointer fingers together
or clap hands.

✿ Similar signs
There is some overlap between this version of the sign
for **CAREFUL** (with hands knocking together) and the
sign for **BABYSITTER** (page 120, with hands circling).

pay attention

Hold your flat hands at the sides of your
face with palms facing each other, and move
both hands straight out in front of you and
back twice.

✳ Memory tip
It's like you're blocking out distractions so you
can focus.

☺ When to use the sign
Sign **PAY ATTENTION** to encourage your child to
listen to you or someone else.

👁 What to look for
Young children often get this one pretty accurately!

stay

Make a *Y* handshape (page 40) with your dominant hand with the palm facing down, and move your hand away from you at a downward angle.

✳ Memory tip

It's like you're indicating the spot where you want someone or something to stay.

☺ When to use the sign

Sign **STAY** when asking your child to stay in her seat at the dinner table or in the shopping cart seat at the grocery store.

👁 What to look for

Your child might do this sign with her pointer finger or whole hand.

wait

Hold both hands with fingers slightly curved and palms facing up, and wiggle all your fingers.

✳ Memory tip

Think of twiddling your fingers when you're bored while waiting.

☺ When to use the sign

If you're on the phone or finishing a task, you can tell your little one he needs to wait by signing **WAIT**.

👁 What to look for

Your baby might wiggle his fingers or bend his hands repeatedly.

broken

Start with two *S* handshapes (page 39) held in front of your body with palms facing down, and twist your wrists away from each other so that your palms are facing each other.

✳ Memory tip
It's like you're holding a stick and you snap it in half.

☺ When to use the sign
Sign **BROKEN** to help your baby understand why she can't play with a toy.

👁 What to look for
Your child might throw her arms open wide or drop them both straight down.

fire

Start with your open hands in front of your body with palms facing you, then move your hands up and down alternately as your wiggle all your fingers.

✳ Memory tip
It's like the movement of flames in a campfire.

☺ When to use the sign
Sign **FIRE** if you are lighting gas burners on your stove, a fireplace, a barbeque, or an outdoor fire pit.

👁 What to look for
Your child might wiggle or bend his fingers with his palms facing out or down.

wash hands

Place your dominant hand on top of your opposite hand, palms touching, and rub them together as you flip your hands so that your nondominant hand is on top and flip them back again.

✳ Memory tip
This one's easy! It's like rubbing the bar of soap as you wash your hands.

☺ When to use the sign
Sign **WASH HANDS** when you clean your little one's hands with a washcloth or wipe as well as when your toddler starts washing her hands in the sink.

👁 What to look for
Your baby might rub her palms together without rotating her hands.

sick

Bend the middle finger on both hands, and tap the middle finger of your dominant hand on your forehead and the middle finger of your nondominant hand on your belly at the same time twice.

✳ Memory tip
It's like you're showing that your head and your stomach hurt.

☺ When to use the sign
Sign **SICK** when your baby isn't feeling well. Make sure to match your facial expression to this sign. Your face should communicate discomfort if you're sick or concern if your child is sick.

👁 What to look for
Your child might touch his head or belly with his pointer finger.

doctor

Make an *M* handshape (page 39) with your dominant hand, and touch the tips of your first three fingers to the inside of your opposite wrist.

✳ Memory tip
It's like a doctor taking your pulse.

☺ When to use the sign
Sign **DOCTOR** when visiting the pediatrician or when playing with a toy doctor set at home.

👁 What to look for
Your child might tap the back of her wrist with her hand.

✿ Similar signs
Sometimes you see this sign done with all the fingers or with a *D* handshape (page 38) for *doctor*.

medicine

Bend the middle finger of your dominant hand and touch it to the open palm of your opposite hand, and rock your dominant hand from side to side a few times.

✳ Memory tip
This represents an old-fashioned mortar and pestle that is still sometimes used to grind and mix medicines.

☺ When to use the sign
Sign **MEDICINE** if your child needs to take a pain reliever, antibiotic, or other medicine.

👁 What to look for
Your baby will likely do this sign with his pointer finger.

SIGNING FUN

Sign and Sing: "Miss Polly Had a Dolly"

"Miss Polly Had a Dolly" is a classic nursery rhyme; however, I didn't learn it until my own kids were in preschool. Once you learn it, it tends to stick in your head, so consider yourself warned. If you're not familiar with the tune, you can find videos on YouTube. It's great for practicing some of the vocabulary we learned in this Health and Safety section!

Key Vocabulary

DOLL, p. 72   **SICK,** p. 137   **DOCTOR,** p. 138

DOOR, p. 116   **BED,** p. 18   **PAPER,** p. 145

MEDICINE, p. 138   **MORNING,** p. 52

Miss Polly had a **DOLLY** who was **SICK**, **SICK**, **SICK**

So she called for the **DOCTOR** to come quick, quick, quick

The **DOCTOR** came with his bag and his hat

And he knocked on the **DOOR** with a rat-a-tat-tat

He looked at the **DOLLY** and he shook his head

And he said, "Miss Polly, put her straight to **BED**!"

He wrote out a **PAPER** for a **PILL**, **PILL**, **PILL** [sign **MEDICINE**]

I'll be back in the **MORNING** with my bill, bill, bill.

Sign and Read: *Llama Llama Home with Mama* by Anna Dewdney

From the popular *Llama Llama* series by the late Anna Dewdney, this installment finds little Llama feeling rotten with a bad cold. We follow Llama's sick day at home with his mama as she takes care of him and slowly comes down with a cold herself. It's a great book for practicing many of the signs you learned in this section. This book is also a wonderful lesson in compassion as little Llama realizes his mama could use some TLC, too!

Key Vocabulary

SICK, p. 137

MOM, p. 26

BED, p. 18

SCHOOL, p. 142

MEDICINE, p. 138

TRUCK, p. 128

TRAIN, p. 31

BOOK, p. 22

SLEEP, p. 51

DRAW, p. 145

TOY, p. 69

RED, p. 155

PILLOW, p. 51

HOME, p. 115

my school

school

Hold your nondominant hand in front of you with palm facing up, and bring your dominant hand down on it so your palms touch twice.

✱ Memory tip
It's like a teacher clapping to get the class to pay attention.

☉ When to use the sign
Sign **SCHOOL** when it's time to go to school. You can use the **SCHOOL** sign when talking about day care as well as preschool or grade school.

👁 What to look for
Your baby might do a regular clap but with a larger motion.

class

Start with both hands in C handshapes (page 38) with palms facing out, then twist your hands so your palms are facing you and your pinky fingers are touching.

✱ Memory tip
C is for *class* surrounding a group of students.

☉ When to use the sign
Sign **CLASS** if your child attends a school with multiple classroom groups. You can ask your child, "Is your friend in your **CLASS** with you?" You can also point to his class picture and sign **CLASS**.

👁 What to look for
Conceptually, this is an advanced sign, but younger children might bring their C hands together in a way that looks similar to the sign for **BALL** (page 22).

❋ Similar signs
There are several signs done with this same motion, but different letter shapes change the meaning. With F hands, it means **FAMILY** (page 118).

teacher

Start with both hands at your temples, with all the fingers of each hand touching, and move your hands forward from your temples away from your head. This is the sign for **TEACH**. Then drop your flat hands with palms facing each other straight down at your sides. This is the sign for **PERSON/AGENT** (see page 132). These signs combined mean **TEACHER**.

✳ Memory tip

Teachers share their knowledge as it comes out from their head into the world.

◎ When to use the sign

If your child has one primary teacher, you can use the sign for **TEACHER** for that teacher's name. For example, you can say, "Miss Courtney is your **TEACHER**. Isn't Miss Courtney [sign **TEACHER**] nice?"

👁 What to look for

Your child might tap her head and then drop her arms.

backpack

Make C handshapes (page 38) with both hands and tap your fingertips twice on the front of your shoulders.

✳ Memory tip

You're showing where your backpack straps would be.

◎ When to use the sign

Sign **BACKPACK** when leaving for or picking up your child from school: "Get your **BACKPACK**; it's time to go!"

👁 What to look for

Your baby might pat his chest with open hands.

✿ Similar signs

There are a few ways to sign **BACKPACK**. Another way is to slide your hands up and down where your straps would be. One more way is to pat your own back with your dominant hand.

read

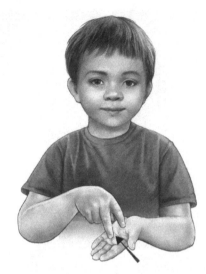

Make a *V* handshape (page 39) with your dominant hand and move your fingertips down your opposite open palm.

✳ **Memory tip**
It's like your fingers are your eyes moving over the page.

🕚 **When to use the sign**
When you see your child turning pages in a book, you can ask, "Are you **READING** that **BOOK** (page 22)? Do you want to **READ** it to me?"

👁 **What to look for**
Your baby might move her pointer finger over her opposite hand.

write

Pinch the pointer finger and thumb of your dominant hand together and move them across your opposite open palm.

✳ **Memory tip**
It's like you're holding a pen and writing.

🕚 **When to use the sign**
When your little one is old enough to try writing letters, you can say, "Can you **WRITE** a letter O for me? It's just like a circle!"

👁 **What to look for**
Your child might tap his pointer finger on his opposite open hand.

draw

Make an *I* handshape (page 38) with your dominant hand and swirl your pinky finger in an *S* pattern on your opposite open palm.

✳ Memory tip

It's like you're drawing on a canvas.

◎ When to use the sign

Sign **DRAW** when your child is playing with crayons or markers. Or ask her, "Would you like to **DRAW**?" as you show her the crayons at home or in a restaurant.

◉ What to look for

Your child might swirl her pointer finger over her opposite open hand.

paper

Hold your nondominant hand in front of you with the palm up and the wrist slightly higher than the fingers, and then slide your dominant hand across your opposite hand, moving from fingers to wrist twice in an upward motion.

✳ Memory tip

It's like paper running through an old-fashioned printing press.

◎ When to use the sign

Ask your child, "Do you need more **PAPER**?" when he is drawing and runs out of space.

◉ What to look for

It might look like your baby is clapping.

pencil

Pinch the pointer finger and thumb of your dominant hand together, hold your hand near your mouth, and then lower it to move it across your opposite open palm.

✶ Memory tip
It's like you're licking the tip of a pencil and then writing.

☉ When to use the sign
Sign **PENCIL** to specify a **PENCIL** versus a **CRAYON** (page 150).

◉ What to look for
Your child might put her pointer finger in her mouth and then move it across her open hand.

scissors

Make a *V* handshape (page 39) with your dominant hand, and open and close your pointer and middle fingers together twice.

✶ Memory tip
It's like your fingers are the scissors.

☉ When to use the sign
Introduce the sign for **SCISSORS** when your older toddler or preschooler is ready to try cutting paper.

◉ What to look for
Your baby might open and close his whole hand or all his fingers.

✿ Similar signs
Whereas you open and close your fingers twice to sign **SCISSORS**, you close your fingers together once to sign **CUT**. This is a noun/verb pair (see page 123).

time

Touch the pointer finger of your dominant hand to the back of your opposite wrist.

✱ Memory tip
It's like you're pointing to your watch.

☺ When to use the sign
You can use **TIME** in conjunction with other signs, like to say "**TIME** for **BED** (page 18)" or to tell your little one "It's not **TIME** yet" when she is anxious to do something.

👁 What to look for
Your baby might touch her wrist or arm with her whole hand.

playground

Make *Y* handshapes (page 40) with both hands and twist them away from each other to sign **PLAY**, then circle your dominant open hand with palm down in the space in front of you to sign **GROUND**. Combine the two signs to sign **PLAYGROUND**.

✱ Memory tip
It's like you're showing the area where you can play.

☺ When to use the sign
Sign **PLAYGROUND** when you're going to visit a local park with your little one.

👁 What to look for
Toddlers often sign **PLAY** by waving their pointer fingers in the air, and **GROUND** might be more of a sweeping motion than a circle.

SIGNING FUN

Sign and Sing: "Mary Had a Little Lamb"

"Mary Had a Little Lamb" is a classic nursery rhyme for children, but we often hear just the first verse. The second verse offers a great opportunity to practice the sign for **SCHOOL**, and it makes the song a lot more fun. Feel free to substitute the sign for **GIRL** in place of Mary's name in the tune if you'd like. In ASL, **LAMB** is usually signed as a combination of the signs **BABY** and **SHEEP**, but since the lyrics already say *little*, we'll sign **LITTLE SHEEP** instead to avoid confusion.

Key Vocabulary

GIRL, p. 121   **LITTLE,** p. 103   **SHEEP,** p. 35

GO, p. 104   **SCHOOL,** p. 142   **DAY,** p. 52

LAUGH, p. 84   **PLAY,** p. 30

Mary [sign **GIRL**] had a **LITTLE LAMB**

LITTLE LAMB, **LITTLE LAMB**

MARY had a **LITTLE LAMB**

Its fleece was white as snow.

And everywhere that **MARY** went

MARY went, **MARY** went

Everywhere that **MARY** went

The **LAMB** was sure to **GO**.

He followed her to **SCHOOL** one **DAY**

SCHOOL one **DAY**, **SCHOOL** one **DAY**

He followed her to **SCHOOL** one **DAY**

Which was against the rule.

It made the children **LAUGH** and **PLAY**

LAUGH and **PLAY**, **LAUGH** and **PLAY**

It made the children **LAUGH** and **PLAY**

To see a **LAMB** at **SCHOOL**.

Sign and Read: *Pete the Cat: Rocking in My School Shoes* by James Dean and Eric Litwin

Pete the Cat rocks! If you're new to the *Pete the Cat* series, you're in for a real treat. Pete the Cat is a wonderful character for teaching kids about the importance of being flexible and going with the flow when things don't go your way. In this particular book, Pete goes to school and learns all about the different areas of the school building, including the classroom, library, playground, and more. You'll have lots of opportunity to practice your school signs together in this fun-to-read-aloud book!

Key Vocabulary

CAT, p. 21   **SCHOOL,** p. 142   **MUSIC,** p. 32

TEACHER, p. 143   **LIBRARY,** p. 126   **READ,** p. 144

EAT, p. 16   **TABLE,** p. 117   **CHAIR,** p. 117

SLIDE, p. 69   **PLAYGROUND,** p. 147   **RUN,** p. 96

WRITE, p. 144   **HOME,** p. 115   **MOM,** p. 26

Advanced Signing: Combining Signs

Combining signs is a great way to take your sign language skills up a notch and teach your little one new signs! Sometimes, combining signs makes a new word, while other times it creates a short phrase. Here are two new signs you can do by combining signs you've already learned.

To sign **RECESS**, combine the signs for **PLAY** and **TIME**.

To sign **CRAYON**, combine the signs for **COLORS** and **WRITE**.

Key Vocabulary

PLAY, p. 30

TIME, p. 147

COLORS, p. 155

WRITE, p. 144

The Big, Wide World

AS PARENTS OR CAREGIVERS, watching the little ones we love discover the world around them can be as fun for us as it is for them. Imagine discovering, touching, and smelling grass for the first time, or seeing your first rainbow!

At birth, babies can see only in black, white, and shades of gray, but over the first few months of life, their vision develops rapidly and they are able to see a full spectrum of color by about 5 months old. At around 18 months, toddlers start identifying colors, usually by responding to questions like "Can you get the blue ball?" by picking up and handing you the requested item. With signing, toddlers can participate even more actively in conversations about colors. In this chapter, you'll learn how to sign all the colors of the rainbow (and then some!) and explore some fun ways to help your little one learn to identify colors.

When I ask the families I work with what kinds of things their children are most interested in, animals almost always make the list. Animals are fun and fascinating to young children and are easily found in nearly every children's book. This chapter includes some of my personal favorite signs to teach children, including **GORILLA** (page 166), **PENGUIN** (page 167), **TURTLE** (page 168), and many more. A trip to the zoo is enhanced tremendously when your child can name the animals he sees with signs. Animal signs are great for playing, reading, and singing with your child, and so you'll find some great activities, books to read, and songs in the pages ahead.

Finally, the great outdoors in general offers many opportunities to explore and expand your child's interests and vocabulary. Read ahead to learn how to sign **ROCK** (page 181) and **LEAF** (page 179) so you can introduce them the next time you're exploring at the park or even in your own backyard!

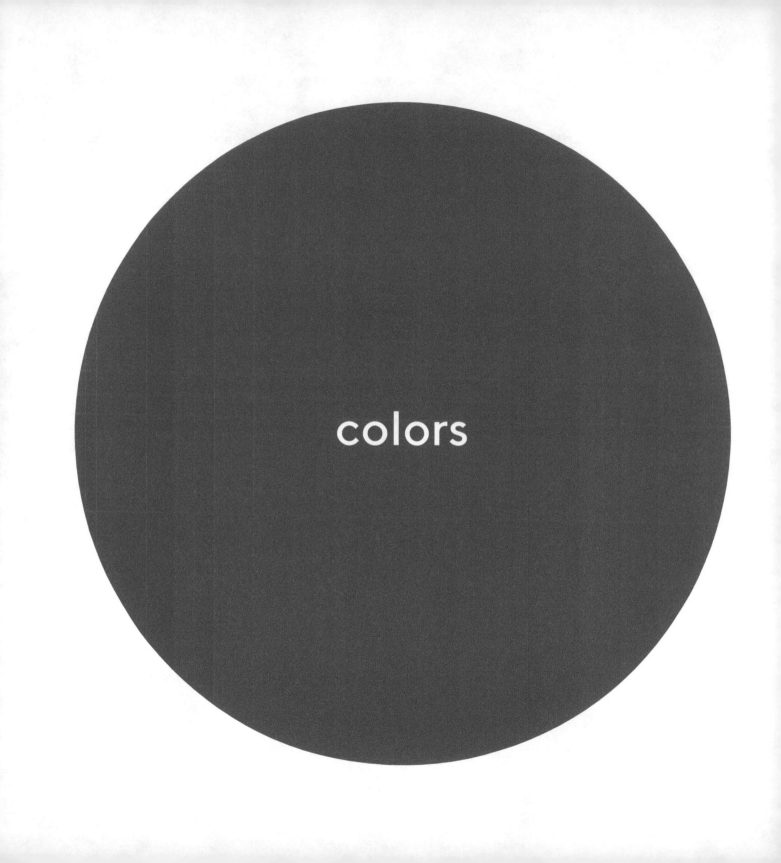

colors

colors

Hold your open hand in front of your neck with palm facing you, and wiggle all your fingertips in front of your chin.

✳ Memory tip
Think of all the different colors of skin in the world.

◌ When to use the sign
When your child has an item with multiple colors, like a box of **CRAYONS** (page 150) or a **TOY** (page 69) with multiple colored **BALLS** (page 22), you can say, "Look at all the pretty **COLORS**! Which **COLOR** do you want?" When your little one picks a crayon or ball, you can teach him the sign for that particular color. "You picked the **GREEN** (page 157) one. I like **GREEN,** too!"

👁 What to look for
Your baby might open and close his hand in front of his neck or face.

red

Touch your pointer finger to your bottom lip and bend it into an *X* handshape (page 39) as it slides down your chin.

✳ Memory tip
You're showing your red lips.

◌ When to use the sign
Sign **RED** when you see a red fire truck or a red tomato.

👁 What to look for
It might look like your baby is pointing to her face or mouth.

*On a walk in our neighborhood, my younger daughter excitedly signed **RED** when she saw a **RED** fire hydrant. I didn't know a sign for fire hydrant, but because we knew our colors, we could still talk about the fire hydrant that she was so interested in.*

orange

Open and close your fist under your chin.

✳ Memory tip
It's like you're squeezing a juicy orange.

◔ When to use the sign
Sign **ORANGE** when eating an orange or when coloring with an orange crayon.

◉ What to look for
It might look like your baby is signing **MILK** (page 16) as the movement is the same, but the location of the sign is different.

❋ Similar signs
The sign is same for both the color orange and the fruit.

yellow

Make a *Y* handshape (page 40) with your dominant hand with your palm facing you, and twist it away from you twice.

✳ Memory tip
Y is for *yellow*.

◔ When to use the sign
Sign **YELLOW** when pointing out the yellow sun in a book or pretty yellow flowers in the **SPRING** (page 182).

◉ What to look for
Younger babies might do this sign with just their pointer finger extended.

❋ Similar signs
If you do this sign with both hands, it is the sign for **PLAY**.

green

Make a *G* handshape (page 38) with your
dominant hand and twist it away from
you twice.

✳ Memory tip
G is for *green*.

☺ When to use the sign
Sign **GREEN** when pointing out the green trees or
when coloring green grass in a drawing.

👁 What to look for
Your baby might twist his closed hand or a *1* handshape (page 40)

blue

Make a *B* handshape (page 38) with your
dominant hand and twist it away from
you twice.

✳ Memory tip
B is for *blue*.

☺ When to use the sign
Sign **BLUE** when pointing out the **BLUE SKY**
(page 179) in a picture book. You can combine the
signs **BLUE** and **BERRY** (page 59) to specify
BLUEBERRIES as opposed to other berries.

👁 What to look for
It might look like your baby is waving.

purple

Make a *P* handshape (page 39) with your dominant hand and twist it away from you twice.

✳ **Memory tip**
P is for *purple*.

🕐 **When to use the sign**
Sign **PURPLE** when coloring with a purple crayon, or ask your child to point to the color **PURPLE** in a rainbow.

👁 **What to look for**
The letter *P* is a pretty tricky one! Younger children might do this by shaking their hand with their pointer finger extended or maybe with a *V* hand-shape (page 39) if they are able.

pink

Touch the middle finger of your *P* hand (page 39) to your lower lip and slide it from your chin.

✳ **Memory tip**
P is for *pink*, like your lips.

🕐 **When to use the sign**
Comment on your child's pretty **PINK** dress or shoes or a friend's **PINK** clothes when you see them.

👁 **What to look for**
It might look very similar to the sign for **RED** (page 155).

🧩 **Similar signs**
PINK is similar to the sign for **RED** (page 155), except it's done with a *P* handshape (page 39) instead of an *X* handshape (page 39).

brown

Start with your *B* hand (page 38) next to your face with palm facing away from you, and slide it down the side of your face.

✳ Memory tip

B is for *brown*, like the skin on your face.

☺ When to use the sign

Point out the **BROWN** dirt or the **BROWN DOG** (page 21) when playing outside with your child.

👁 What to look for

It might look like your baby is wiping her face.

black

Touch your pointer finger to the end of your opposite eyebrow, and slide your pointer across both eyebrows.

✳ Memory tip

Think of drawing a line to show your black eyebrows.

☺ When to use the sign

Talk about the **BLACK CAR** (page 23) or **BLACK CAT** (page 21) with your child.

👁 What to look for

Babies might drag their pointer across their fore-head, cheek, or chin when they sign **BLACK**.

white

Place your dominant open hand on your chest. Pull your hand away from your body and close your fingers to your thumb.

✳ Memory tip
It's like you're showing your nice **WHITE** shirt.

☺ When to use the sign
Talk about the plain **WHITE PAPER** (page 145) before you and your child draw on it, and then talk about all the **COLORS** (page 155) after your little one has drawn all over it.

👁 What to look for
Your child might grab at his shirt.

SIGNING FUN

Sign and Play: What Color Is It?

Fill an empty baby wipe container or tissue box with items of multiple colors. You can use small balls or colored tissue paper cut into smaller pieces. Encourage your child to reach in and pull something out of the box. Then ask, "What **COLOR** is it?" Pause to give your child a chance to guess the color. If he's still learning colors, you can teach him the word and the sign. You can say, "You found some **YELLOW** tissue! Can you sign **YELLOW**?" Repeat for as long as your child is interested. As you pull items out of the box, you can sort them by color to reinforce the concept.

Key Vocabulary

COLORS, p. 155

RED, p. 155

ORANGE, p. 156

YELLOW, p. 156

GREEN, p. 157

BLUE, p. 157

PURPLE, p. 158

Sign and Read: *Dog's Colorful Day: A Messy Story about Colors and Counting* by Emma Dodd

This is a wonderful book for learning about colors and numbers. *Dog's Colorful Day* is a story about a white dog with one black spot. But as he moves through his day, he picks up more and more spots of different colors. With each new spot, you can introduce the color and its sign. You can also practice counting over and over as the number of spots grows. By the end of the day, Dog has 10 spots of different colors, but after a nice bath, he goes back to just the one black spot that belongs to him!

Key Vocabulary

DOG, p. 21   **WHITE,** p. 160   **BLACK,** p. 159

RED, p. 155   **BLUE,** p. 157   **GREEN,** p. 157

BROWN, p. 159   **PURPLE,** p. 158   **BATH,** p. 19

GOOD, p. 109   **NIGHT,** p. 53

animals

animal

Place the fingertips of each hand on the front of your shoulders and move your elbows forward and back.

✳ Memory tip
Think of a bird flapping its wings.

☺ When to use the sign
ANIMAL is a useful sign when you want to talk about an animal but don't know the sign for it. You can say the name of the animal and use the **ANIMAL** sign, too. For example, "Look at that tall giraffe! A giraffe is an **ANIMAL** that lives in Africa."

👁 What to look for
Your child might "flap" her elbows up and down instead of forward and back.

chicken

With your dominant hand, open and close your pointer finger to your thumb in front of your mouth. Then, tap your pointer finger and thumb to your opposite open palm.

✳ Memory tip
Picture a chicken's beak opening and closing and then pecking the ground.

☺ When to use the sign
Sign **CHICKEN** when visiting a farm or if you have your own chickens!

👁 What to look for
Babies often open and close their whole hand or open and close their pointer and thumb away from their face.

✸ Similar signs
CHICKEN is sometimes signed with just the first part in front of the mouth, which is also the sign for **BIRD**.

goat

Make an *S* hand (page 39) and touch it to your chin with your palm toward your face, and then make a slightly bent *V* hand (page 39) and touch it to your forehead with your palm still toward your face.

✱ Memory tip
You're showing the goat's beard and horns.

☺ When to use the sign
Sign **GOAT** when reading a story about farm animals. Point out the goat's horns and then show your baby the sign.

👁 What to look for
Babies might tap their closed fist to their cheek or the top of their head.

❋ Similar signs
Sometimes **GOAT** is signed with a bent *V* hand at both the chin and the forehead.

alligator

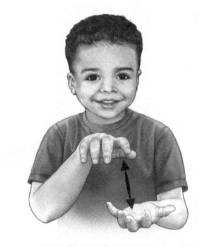

Reach both arms in front of you with palms facing each other and fingers slightly bent, and open and close your hands together twice.

✱ Memory tip
Your fingers are like an alligator's teeth in its big, chomping mouth.

☺ When to use the sign
Sign **ALLIGATOR** when you sign and sing "Five Little Monkeys Swinging in a Tree" (page 174).

👁 What to look for
It might look like an exaggerated clap.

❋ Similar signs
Use this sign for both **ALLIGATOR** and **CROCODILE**.

elephant

Start with your flat dominant hand in front of your nose and move it down and away from your face.

✳ Memory tip
You're showing an elephant's long trunk.

☺ When to use the sign
Sign **ELEPHANT** when visiting a zoo or circus or when reading a book about wild animals. Talk about the elephant's big ears and long trunk. Talking about elephants is also a great time to practice the sign for **BIG** (page 103)!

◉ What to look for
Your baby might swing his arm around and pretend to be an elephant!

✿ Similar signs
ELEPHANT is also signed with the same motion but with a C handshape (page 38).

gorilla

Make a fist with both hands and thump your chest with your hands alternately.

✳ Memory tip
It's like you're a gorilla beating its chest.

☺ When to use the sign
Sign **GORILLA** when reading Good Night, Gorilla by Peggy Rathmann (page 175) to your little one.

◉ What to look for
Your little one might thump both hands at the same time before learning how to switch them back and forth.

As a toddler, my daughter was really interested in the patio furniture when we first put it out. I commented, "Are you looking at the table and umbrella?" She then signed **GORILLA**. I never thought of gorilla and umbrella sounding the same until that moment! I then told her the new word more clearly—that's called an "UM-brel-la."

penguin

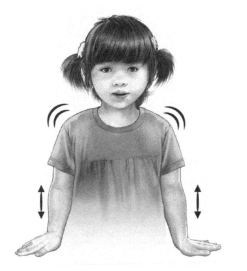

Hold both arms straight at your sides with your wrists bent so your palms are facing the floor, then tilt your torso side to side.

✳ Memory tip
It's a like a penguin waddling.

☺ When to use the sign
There are a number of cute movies about penguins for young children, including *Happy Feet* and *March of the Penguins*. You can teach the sign for **PEN-GUIN** when watching a film or visiting an aquarium.

👁 What to look for
This might be one of my favorite signs to see little ones do—it's the cutest!

tiger

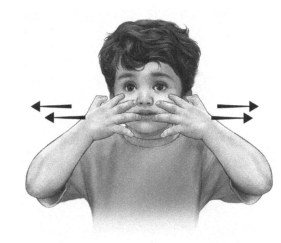

Hold your open hands with slightly curved fingers in front of your face with fingertips touching, and then move both hands away from each other twice.

✳ Memory tip
You're showing the stripes on a tiger's face.

☺ When to use the sign
Sign **TIGER** if you go to the zoo or if your child has a stuffed or toy tiger that he likes to play with.

👁 What to look for
Your baby might drag his hands down his face.

zebra

Hold your open hands with slightly curved fingers in front of your torso with fingertips touching, and then move both hands away from each other twice.

✳ Memory tip
You're showing the stripes on a zebra's coat.

☺ When to use the sign
Sign **ZEBRA** when reading a book that features a zebra.

👁 What to look for
Your baby might swipe one or two flat hands across her body.

turtle

Make a thumbs-up with your dominant hand with the thumb pointing away from you, and place your bent nondominant hand over the base of your dominant thumb, and then wiggle your thumb.

✳ Memory tip
It's like your thumb is a turtle's head and your top hand is its shell.

☺ When to use the sign
Sign **TURTLE** when visiting a pet shop or reading the classic story about the tortoise and the hare.

👁 What to look for
Little ones might clasp their hands together and wiggle their fingers.

squirrel

Make a bent *V* handshape (page 39) with both hands and hold them in front of your chest with palms facing, then tap your bent *V* fingertips together a few times.

✱ Memory tip

Think of a squirrel munching on an acorn.

☺ When to use the sign

Depending on where you live, squirrels are often easy to find. Teach your child the sign for **SQUIRREL** in your backyard, a schoolyard, on a nature trail, or at a local park.

👁 What to look for

Babies might tap all their fingertips together or do a gentle clapping motion.

owl

Hold two O handshapes (page 39) in front of your eyes and twist them away from each other twice.

✱ Memory tip

You're showing an owl's big eyes.

☺ When to use the sign

Lots of toys and decorations have owls on them. Point out the owl on your child's dishes, shirt, towel, or other item and say, "Look at that **OWL**—the **OWL** says hoo hoo!"

👁 What to look for

This is another one that is super cute when little ones do it.

raccoon

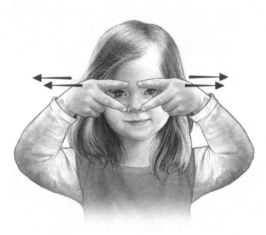

Hold two *V* handshapes (page 39) sideways in front of your eyes with palms toward your face. Then move both hands apart, away from your eyes, as you close your fingers into *U* handshapes (page 39).

✳ Memory tip
You're showing the black stripe over a raccoon's eyes.

☺ When to use the sign
Sign **RACCOON** when reading a book about forest animals or if your child has a stuffed raccoon toy.

👁 What to look for
Your child might wipe his eyelids with his fingertips.

wolf

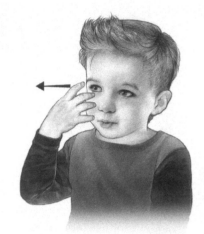

Start with your dominant relaxed hand in front of your face with the palm toward your nose, then move your hand straight out from your nose while bringing your fingertips to your thumb.

✳ Memory tip
You're showing the large snout of a wolf.

☺ When to use the sign
Sign **WOLF** when reading classic stories like *Little Red Riding Hood* and *The Three Little Pigs*.

👁 What to look for
It might look like your baby is grabbing at her nose or cheek.

snake

Make a bent *V* handshape (page 39) and hold it in front of your mouth with your palm facing out, and then move your hand away from you in a curving motion.

✳ Memory tip
Your fingers are a snake's forked tongue, and your arm moves in the curving pattern of a snake.

◉ When to use the sign
Sign **SNAKE** if you see some snakes at the pet shop. Pair this sign with a hissing sound—your child just might mimic you!

◉ What to look for
Your child might wave his pointer finger and even make a "sssssss" sound if you model the sound with the sign.

worm

Hold your nondominant flat hand with palm facing out and place the pointer finger of your dominant hand flat against your opposite palm. Bend and straighten your pointer finger as you move from the wrist to fingertips of your opposite hand.

✳ Memory tip
It's like a worm squirming through the ground.

◉ When to use the sign
If you find a worm on a rainy-day walk or in the backyard, you can show your little one the sign for **WORM**.

◉ What to look for
It might look like your child is scratching her other hand.

caterpillar

Hold your nondominant arm in front of your body with elbow bent and palm facing the floor, and place your dominant hand with pointer finger extended on the back of your opposite wrist, then bend and straighten your pointer finger as you move your hand from your wrist toward your elbow.

✳ Memory tip

It's like a little caterpillar is crawling up your arm.

☺ When to use the sign

Teach your baby the sign for **CATERPILLAR** when reading *The Very Hungry Caterpillar* by Eric Carle.

👁 What to look for

It might look like your baby is scratching his arm.

shark

Make a *B* handshape (page 38) and place the base of your thumb at the top of your forehead.

✳ Memory tip

It's like a shark's fin sticking up through the water.

☺ When to use the sign

Have fun signing **SHARK** at the aquarium or at home, singing the "Baby Shark" song with your little one.

👁 What to look for

Your baby may pat or point to her head.

🧩 Similar signs

There is another version of **SHARK**, in which you hold your nondominant hand in front of you with palm facing down, place your *B* hand behind it, and move them away from you together. Your nondominant hand represents the water surface, and your *B* hand is the shark's fin.

whale

Make a *Y* handshape (page 40) with your dominant hand and reach it across your body with the palm down, then move your hand back toward your dominant side as you bend your wrist up and down a few times.

✳ Memory tip
Imagine your pinky and thumb are a whale's large tail fin splashing in the water.

☺ When to use the sign
If you have a whale bath toy, you can teach your child to sign **WHALE** as he plays and splashes in the tub.

👁 What to look for
Your child might move his fist up and down in a large motion.

✳ Similar signs
Sometimes **WHALE** is signed with one big splashing motion.

octopus

Hold your dominant hand in front of you with fingers open loosely and palm facing down. Place the fingertips of your nondominant hand on the back of your dominant hand and then wiggle the fingers of your dominant hand.

✳ Memory tip
Your top hand is an octopus's body and your bottom hand is its tentacles.

☺ When to use the sign
Sign **OCTOPUS** (along with **SHARK** [page 172] and **WHALE** [page 173]) when reading a book about the ocean, like *Commotion in the Ocean* by Giles Andreae.

👁 What to look for
I've seen preschool-age kids do a fantastic version of this sign.

Sign and Sing: "Five Little Monkeys Swinging in a Tree"

This is a fun and cheeky song about naughty monkeys who keep teasing Mr. Alligator. One by one, Mr. Alligator teaches those naughty monkeys a lesson . . . until the last one, who learns he'd better leave Mr. Alligator alone! I love to do a big "snap" with my **ALLIGATOR** arms each time the words in the song say "snap." It's a very effective way to show how this sign represents a big, hungry alligator!

Key Vocabulary

MONKEY, p. 35   **TREE,** p. 32   **ALLIGATOR,** p. 165

ONE, p. 40   **TWO,** p. 40   **THREE,** p. 40

FOUR, p. 40   **FIVE,** p. 40

FIVE little **MONKEYS** swinging in a **TREE**

Teasing Mr. **ALLIGATOR**

"You can't catch me! You can't catch me!"

Along came Mr. **ALLIGATOR,** as quiet as can be

And snapped [sign **ALLIGATOR**] that monkey right out of the **TREE.**

FOUR little **MONKEYS** swinging in a **TREE**

Teasing Mr. **ALLIGATOR**

"You can't catch me! You can't catch me!"

Along came Mr. **ALLIGATOR,** as quiet as can be

And snapped [sign **ALLIGATOR**] that monkey right out of the **TREE.**

THREE little **MONKEYS** swinging in a **TREE** [. . .]

TWO little **MONKEYS** swinging in a **TREE** [. . .]

ONE little **MONKEY** swinging in a **TREE** [. . .]

Teasing Mr. **ALLIGATOR**

"You can't catch me! You can't catch me!"

Along came Mr. **ALLIGATOR,** as quiet as can be

And the **MONKEY** cried out, "Ha, ha! Missed me!"

Sign and Read: *Good Night, Gorilla* by Peggy Rathmann

This popular little board book has very few words, which actually makes for great language-building fun with your little one! The story follows a zookeeper locking up and saying "good night" to all the animals, but a very mischievous gorilla makes the evening a *lot* more interesting. What I love about this book is the opportunity to tell the story differently each time. My older daughter loved this book and would point out the balloon that floats away and the little mouse with the big banana on each page. If you look closely, you'll see that each of the animals in the zoo has a toy version of itself in its cage, which is also a fun conversation point and provides the opportunity to practice the sign. I think our favorite spread in the book is the one with all the good-night word bubbles in the dark. We had so much fun saying "good night" in what we imagined all the animal's voices sounded like. Maybe this one will become a favorite in your house, too!

Key Vocabulary

GOOD, p. 109

NIGHT, p. 53

GORILLA, p. 166

MOUSE, p. 34

ELEPHANT, p. 166

BALLOON, p. 75

BANANA, p. 34

HOUSE, p. 115

BED, p. 18

LIGHT, p. 23

SLEEP, p. 51

wind

Hold both hands in front of your body with palms facing and move them loosely from side to side in unison.

✳ Memory tip

It's like the wind is blowing your hands back and forth.

◎ When to use the sign

Show your child the sign for **WIND** when you see her react to the breeze against her face. You can even make your own wind with an electric or handheld fan.

👁 What to look for

Little ones usually swing their whole arms from side to side in an exaggerated way.

snow

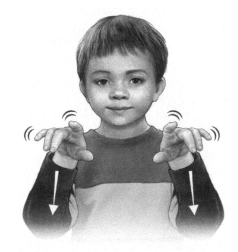

Hold your open hands with palms down in front of your face, and wiggle all your fingers as you slowly lower your hands toward the floor.

✳ Memory tip

You're showing snowflakes slowly fluttering to the ground.

◎ When to use the sign

Sign **SNOW** if you have the opportunity to play in the snow with your child. If it doesn't snow where you live, you can point out the snow in a book, like *The Snowy Day* by Ezra Jack Keats.

👁 What to look for

It might look like your baby is waving with both hands.

cloud

Hold both hands near the top of your head with fingers loosely bent and palms facing. Rotate your hands in a circular manner as you move them across the space in front of your forehead.

✳ Memory tip
You're showing the soft shapes of clouds in the sky.

☺ When to use the sign
Point to the different clouds in the sky to teach your child the sign for **CLOUD**. You can also practice the sign for **CLOUD** while reading *It Looked Like Spilt Milk* by Charles G. Shaw (page 184).

👁 What to look for
This sign requires a fairly high level of coordination so it might be harder to recognize. Babies might look like they are batting the air.

✺ Similar signs
CLOUD is also signed with the hands facing each other vertically and moving them around to show the shape of one fluffy cloud.

rainbow

Reach your dominant hand across your body and, with a 4 handshape (page 40) with palm facing you, make an arc in the space in front of your chest.

✳ Memory tip
Your fingers are showing the colors as you show the shape of a rainbow.

☺ When to use the sign
If you don't get the chance to spot a rainbow in nature, draw one on paper. Point out each of the beautiful **COLORS** (page 155) while you're at it!

👁 What to look for
Babies do a good job of moving their hands through the air for this sign, but it might be hard to distinguish from **SKY** (page 179).

sky

Reach your dominant flat hand across your body and move it in an arc over your head.

✱ Memory tip
Your hand is showing the sky above your head.

◎ When to use the sign
I like to use the sign **SKY** when singing "Twinkle, Twinkle Little Star" with children in my classes, at the end of the line "...like a diamond in the **SKY**."

◉ What to look for
SKY and **RAINBOW** (page 178) use different handshapes, and **SKY** is done higher up above the head, but the two signs can still look similar when done by little hands. Use the context of the situation to help you identify which sign your child is doing.

leaf

Hold your dominant hand with palm down and fingers open and loosely bent. Place the pointer finger of your nondominant hand on the inside of your dominant wrist and then gently shake your open hand from side to side.

✱ Memory tip
It's like a leaf on a tree gently blowing in the breeze.

◎ When to use the sign
If you find a leaf on the ground, show it to your little one and show her the sign for **LEAF**. If you can find leaves with different colors and shapes, you can play a sorting game to sort the ones that are **SAME** (page 107) and **DIFFERENT** (page 107). In the autumn, this is a fun one to repeat as you find leaves falling down.

◉ What to look for
Toddlers often place their pointer finger on the back of their wrist (instead of inside the wrist) when doing this sign, which is just fine!

grass

Make a "claw" hand (fingers open and curved) with your dominant hand and brush your palm under and away from your chin twice.

✳ Memory tip
Think of a cow munching on the grass.

🕐 When to use the sign
Grass can be a big sensory experience for young children—some babies don't mind it, while others aren't so crazy about it. If your child is hesitant about the experience, let him sit on a small blanket and explore the grass around him from the safety of the blanket. You can even pull a few blades of grass out and let him hold them in his hand. Take this opportunity to introduce the sign for **GRASS**.

👁 What to look for
Your child might touch the back of his hand to his chin or cheek.

stream

Hold your flat hands at your sides with palms facing each other, then move your hands away from your body in unison in a curvy motion.

✳ Memory tip
You're showing the winding path of a stream.

🕐 When to use the sign
Sign **STREAM** when you find a little path of water outdoors or even water running along the curb. You can also sign **STREAM** when singing "Row, Row, Row Your Boat" (page 131).

👁 What to look for
Your baby might wave her hands from side to side in a way that looks similar to **ALL DONE** (page 18).

rock

Make two *S* hands (page 39) with palms facing the floor, and tap your dominant hand on the back of your nondominant hand twice.

✳ Memory tip
It's like you're banging one rock on top of another rock.

☺ When to use the sign
Sign **ROCK** if you find a little pebble or see a big boulder outside. You can use the signs for **BIG** (page 103) and **LITTLE** (page 103) to differentiate the rocks you find.

👁 What to look for
Your baby might bang his fists together in a way that looks similar to the sign for **MORE** (page 17).

✿ Similar signs
ROCK is very similar to the sign for **WORK** (page 128), except **WORK** is signed closer to the wrist and **ROCK** is signed on the back of the lower hand.

summer

Reach the pointer finger of your dominant hand to the opposite side of your forehead, and pull your pointer finger across your forehead, bending your pointer finger as you finish.

✳ Memory tip
Think of wiping the sweat from your brow.

☺ When to use the sign
Sign **SUMMER** when talking to your child about the seasons in the year. Read a book about things you can do in the summer, like *Baby Loves Summer* by Karen Katz or *At the Beach* by Anne Rockwell.

👁 What to look for
Baby might wipe her forehead or cheek with her whole hand.

✿ Similar signs
The sign for **SUMMER** is similar to the sign for **BLACK** (page 159), except the pointer finger bends when signing **SUMMER**.

winter

Hold your arms close to your body with closed fists and shake them quickly.

✱ **Memory tip**
It's like you're shivering from the cold.

☺ **When to use the sign**
Since the sign for **WINTER** is the same as the sign for **COLD**, you can teach this sign at a natural opportunity when your child is shivering, like when he just comes out of the bathtub. Then practice the sign when reading a book about things you can do in the winter, like *The Mitten* by Jan Brett or *Snowmen at Night* by Caralyn and Mark Buehner.

👁 **What to look for**
Even young babies get this one just right, and it's usually spot on!

spring

Wrap your nondominant hand around the fingers of your dominant hand with the fingers pointing up, then slide your dominant hand up so your nondominant hand ends up wrapped around your wrist. Open the fingers of your dominant hand as it moves up through your opposite hand.

✱ **Memory tip**
It's like a flower pushing up through the dirt.

☺ **When to use the sign**
Use this sign on an outing to the park, where you can use it with **GRASS** (page 180), **SQUIRREL** (page 169), and **WORM** (page 171).

👁 **What to look for**
Baby might grab his wrist or making a wiping motion on his opposite arm.

✿ **Similar signs**
To sign **GARDEN**, repeat the sign for **SPRING** two more times as you move both hands across the space in front of your body, like a row of flowers blooming.

autumn

Hold your nondominant arm at an upward angle in front of your chest, and brush your dominant hand down your opposite forearm toward the elbow two times.

✻ Memory tip

It's like leaves falling off a tree.

☺ When to use the sign

Sign **AUTUMN** when playing outside on a crisp fall day or when reading a book about the season, like *Apples and Pumpkins* by Anne and Lizzy Rockwell.

👁 What to look for

Younger children might wipe their arm from elbow to wrist.

SIGNING FUN

Sign and Read: *It Looked Like Spilt Milk* by Charles G. Shaw

This book is a wonderful interactive story. Each page features a white shape on a dark background, and you can ask your child what he thinks the shape might be. It's like a book version of finding shapes in the clouds! While the book does tell you what each shape is supposed to look like, there are really no right or wrong answers as you turn the pages and share what you see in each illustration. This book will provide an opportunity to practice many of the signs you have learned in this book as well as some from *Baby Sign Language Made Easy*.

Key Vocabulary

MILK, p. 16   **TREE,** p. 32   **BIRTHDAY,** p. 75

CAKE, p. 64   **SHEEP,** p. 35   **OWL,** p. 169

SQUIRREL, p. 169   **CLOUD,** p. 178

Sign and Sing: "Four Seasons in a Year"

The language and usage of the names of the seasons is something that takes time to master. First, your baby will need to identify basic seasonal words, like **SNOW** (page 177) and **SWIMMING** (page 96), for example. As your child grows and develops, she will begin to understand the concept that certain holidays and activities occur at specific times of the year. As your child grows to preschool age, she can begin to understand that **SNOW** (page 177) falls in the **WINTER** (page 182) or that we go **SWIMMING** (page 96) in the **SUMMER** (page 181). The following simple tune is a good way to introduce this vocabulary and practice the signs.

Key Vocabulary

FOUR, p. 40

SPRING, p. 182

SUMMER, p. 181

AUTUMN, p. 183

WINTER, p. 182

(Sung to the tune of "The Farmer in the Dell")

FOUR seasons in a year

FOUR seasons in a year

WINTER, **SPRING**, **SUMMER**, and **FALL**

FOUR seasons in a year.

In **SPRING** the flowers grow

In **SPRING** the flowers grow

WINTER, **SPRING**, **SUMMER**, and **FALL**

In **SPRING** the flowers grow.

In **SUMMER** it gets so hot [. . .]

In **FALL** the leaves come down [. . .]

In **WINTER** it gets so cold [. . .]

resources

AUTHOR'S WEBSITE

Visit me online for upcoming classes and workshops as well as free helpful videos.

TinySigns.net

ONLINE VIDEO DICTIONARY

You might find it helpful to see the signs you've learned in this book in action. I've created a free video dictionary of all the signs in this book on my Tiny Signs® website, where you can find short videos of me demonstrating each of the signs as well as all the signs from my first book, *Baby Sign Language Made Easy*, and other free bonuses just for book owners!

TinySigns.net/book-owner

ASL WEBSITES

If you'd like to learn more about American Sign Language and the Deaf community, the following sites are a great place to start. You can also search online for any in-person ASL classes that might be offered in your area.

Handspeak.com

Lifeprint.com

SignLanguage101.com

SignItASL.com

SigningOnline.com

StartASL.com

RESEARCH

For findings on the beneficial effects of signs and gestures on infants' language development, see the following.

Baby Signs Too. "The Science behind the Signing." Accessed February 7, 2018. https://www.babysignstoo.com/information /research.

Daniels, Marilyn. *Dancing with Words: Signing for Hearing Children's Literacy*. Westport, CT: Bergin & Garvey, 2000.

Goodwyn, Susan W., Linda P. Acredolo, and Catherine A. Brown. "Impact of Symbolic Gesturing on Early Language Development." *Journal of Verbal and Nonverbal Behavior* 24, no. 2 (2000): 81–103.

Rebelo, Lane. "Using Sign Language with Babies: What the Research Shows." *Tiny Signs*. Accessed February 7, 2018. https://tinysigns .net/baby-sign-language-research/.

Two Little Hands Productions. "Research." *Signing Time*. Accessed February 7, 2018. https://www.signingtime.com/resources/ research.

GREAT PICTURE BOOKS FOR READING AND SIGNING

As you learned throughout this book, story time is a great time to introduce new vocabulary and practice signing with your child. Following is a list of books I love to read and sign with little ones!

Signing Fun Books in *The Complete Guide to Baby Sign Language*

Chicka Chicka Boom Boom by Bill Martin Jr. and John Archambault

Chicka Chicka ABC by Bill Martin Jr. and John Archambault

Goodnight Moon by Margaret Wise Brown

The Little Mouse, the Red Ripe Strawberry, and the Big Hungry Bear by Don and Audrey Wood

Birthday Monsters! by Sandra Boynton

How Does Baby Feel? by Karen Katz

The Way I Feel by Janan Cain

Barnyard Dance! by Sandra Boynton

Llama Llama Home with Mama by Anna Dewdney

Pete the Cat: Rocking in My School Shoes by James Dean and Eric Litwin

Dog's Colorful Day: A Messy Story about Colors and Counting by Emma Dodd

Good Night, Gorilla by Peggy Rathmann

It Looked Like Spilt Milk by Charles G. Shaw

Other Great Books for Signing with Children

The Animal Boogie by Debbie Harter

Apples and Pumpkins by Anne and Lizzy Rockwell

At the Beach by Anne Rockwell

Baby Loves Fall! by Karen Katz

Baby Loves Spring! by Karen Katz

Baby Loves Summer! by Karen Katz

Baby Loves Winter! by Karen Katz

Bear Feels Sick by Karma Wilson and Jane Chapman

Big Little by Leslie Patricelli

Big Red Barn by Margaret Wise Brown

The Birthday Pet by Ellen Javernick and Kevin O'Malley

Commotion in the Ocean by Giles Andreae

Counting Kisses by Karen Katz

The Crayon Box That Talked by Shane Derolf and Michael Letzig

Dragons Love Tacos by Adam Rubin and Daniel Salmieri

I'm the Biggest Thing in the Ocean by Kevin Sherry

Jamberry by Bruce Degen

The Mitten by Jan Brett

Mouse Paint by Ellen Stoll Walsh

No No Yes Yes by Leslie Patricelli

Oh My Oh My Oh Dinosaurs! by Sandra Boynton

One, Two, Three! by Sandra Boynton

Pajama Time! by Sandra Boynton

Pete the Cat: I Love My White Shoes by James Dean and Eric Litwin

A Potty for Me! by Karen Katz

Snowmen All Year by Caralyn and Mark Buehner

Snowmen at Night by Caralyn and Mark Buehner

The Snowy Day by Ezra Jack Keats

Time for Bed by Mem Fox

The Very Busy Spider by Eric Carle

The Very Hungry Caterpillar by Eric Carle

index of signs

index of signs **191**

index

acknowledgments

Thank you to the amazing team at Callisto Media for giving me another opportunity to share my knowledge of baby sign language with parents, caregivers, and educators. A special thank you to my editor, Bridget Fitzgerald, for your help and support throughout the creation of this second book. I have so much appreciation for the talented design team at Callisto, who magically transformed some words on a page into the gorgeous book that you hold in your hands. Thank you!

I want to thank Boris Stoilov, the incredible artist who shared his talent with us in this book and in *Baby Sign Language Made Easy*. You are a gifted illustrator, and we all benefit from your shared talent in these books.

Lastly, I want to thank all the members of the Tiny Signs® community near and far. Whether you took an in-person class or training with me here in Massachusetts a decade ago or just signed up for my online course yesterday, you are like family to me, and it's my privilege and honor to help you succeed with baby sign language. Thank you!

about the author

LANE REBELO, LCSW, is the author of the bestselling *Baby Sign Language Made Easy: 101 Signs to Start Communicating with Your Child Now* and the founder of Tiny Signs®, an award-winning baby sign language program. As a licensed social worker, Lane worked for many years with families in the Boston area. She began studying American Sign Language in 2006 after her first baby was born and was amazed by all she had to say. Lane lives with her husband and two daughters in MetroWest Boston. You can find her online at TinySigns.net.